Other books by Julia Trops

2013 Okanagan Erotic Art Show Catalog
2012 Okanagan Erotic Art Show Catalog
2011 Okanagan Erotic Art Show Catalog
Simplicity in Mind - catalog for the Livessence Society for Figurative
Artists and Models
2009 Okanagan Erotic Art Show Catalog
Lauren - Sensuality of Form

"It is more fun to talk with someone who doesn't use long, difficult words but rather short, easy words like "What about lunch?""

Winnie the Pooh

About the author

Julia Trops is a Canadian artist currently located in the Central Okanagan, in British Columbia, Canada. In her previous life, she was in the military for twelve years, and has three military medals, two for peacekeeping, and one for long service.

Over the past fifteen years, Julia has sold over 1200 works world wide and is deeply involved with her local art community. Often other artists write for guidance and opinion, and due to these many requests, this book was born.

For more on Julia visit her website http://www.juliatrops.com or her online gallery http://www.juliatropsart.com. Julia welcomes gallery representation suggestions.

Art and Money   Electronic book text ISBN 978-0-9813363-6-7
Art and Money   Mass Paperback ISBN 978-0-9813363-5-0

Written and published by Julia Trops

Cover artwork The Choir, acrylic, Julia Trops

Fonts: Adobe Garamond Pro, Arial

Art & Money

by Julia Trops

Table of Contents

Chapter 1 - Who Is This Book For?   1
Chapter 2 - Artists Today   7
Chapter 3 - Why Are You an Artist?   13
Chapter 4 - Do You Have a Map?   25
Chapter 5 - The Paper Toolbox   33
Chapter 6 - Galleries   43
Chapter 7 - The Marketplace   51
Chapter 8 - Showing Your Work   65
Chapter 9 - Pricing Your Artwork   77
Chapter 10 - Cheerleaders   91
Chapter 11 - Charity and Donations   99
Chapter 12 - Art and the Internet   115
Chapter 13 - Photographs   123
Chapter 14 - Businesses and Art   131
Chapter 15 - Spending Money   139
Chapter 16 - The Artist and the City   147
Chapter 17 - Creating Your Event   157
Chapter 18 - Summary   167
Appendix 1 - Recommended Reading   170
Appendix 2 - Arts Funders in Canada(2013)   171

Chapter 1 - Who Is This Book For?

Who Is This Book For?

This book is for artists, like me, whether you want to sell your work or not. I consider myself to be Joe Public professional artist, and I've been asked over and over to give seminars/workshops on what has worked for me and what I have learned over the past 15 years. I'm not a public speaker, and prefer to write, so this is why I am doing this book. I believe in the community of artists, and am happy to help another.

There's lots of books out there on what the "Big" art world is all about, how to get in to it, what to expect. This book is not about that. This book is for Joe Artist, trying to make a living from his or her artwork. It's not how to get in to Tate, or the Met, or be taken in by the big galleries in New York. It's down to earth practical advice as I have experienced it, in a fairly small community. You should be able to take these principles and apply them if you are in a larger city. If you are like me, you will use the info in this book, and the info in other books to help you in your career that is your journey.

I am writing this book as much for me as for you. I believe in what I do, and I believe that you don't need to soak people to help them out. Help and guidance are never over-rated. I am a creative problem solver, and have accomplished a great deal working hard as a full time artist. I listen to others, see what works for them, decide if I want to follow their footsteps, but regardless, recognizing that there are patterns that work. I am not an expert - if I was, I would be a marketer, (and paid much more) - not an artist.

Where I currently live in the Central Okanagan British Columbia, Canada, there are about one hundred and eighty thousand people. Politically, the City of Kelowna is very culturally invested, with a great deal of work which resulted in its being named the Culture Capital of Canada in 2004[1]. Much attention has been given to the area of culture from the city standpoint itself, and it struggles as well to create and identify its own identity and heritage. The city has had the foresight to develop a Cultural Department; not many towns or cities have done that, have made that commitment. If you live in such a city, perhaps that is a way you can participate. More on that later.

1   Cultural Capital of Canada, 2004 Award by Canadian Heritage, Government of Canada

I am not always diplomatic, and some of what I will say is tongue in cheek. I am not writing to be confrontational or mean, but to give you something to think about. Maybe you already know what I am going to say. There are going to be some schools of thought that will have the opinion that what I am going to say is bullshit, or sacrilege, or completely unacceptable.

There are going to be small rants throughout the text in various subject areas. Some of these were taken from my blog, some were written as I was musing about the subjects in this book. Everything I do say in here are factual accounts of interactions with businesses and or individuals. If I refer to my website, it is http://www.juliatrops.com. I've included these because I think many other artists have encountered similar situations, and I want them to know that another artist understands their frustrations or their joy. If I refer to a newspaper article, you can find copies of these on my website.

Looking at the whole picture, it can be overwhelming, so we'll take it one step at a time. Do I say this book is all encompassing? No, absolutely not. There are as many experiences in the world as there are people, and what I am giving you here is mine. It is one person's viewpoint. Question it. Yours may be different, and these experiences may differ according to geographic region, population, type of population and the artist's goals themselves.

Maybe you're the type of person who likes to fly by the seat of your pants, or be footloose and fancy free and can not be troubled to plan for the future. I'd wager too that you would have trouble meeting deadlines, whether self imposed or not. Or maybe you are the kind of person who wants others to do the "work" while you just do the art.

This book is not for you.

This book is for someone who wonders why they are an artist. What on earth were they thinking when they signed up for art workshops, seminars, even university or college. Questions they ask themselves are who, what, where, why and how are they going to function, pay the bills, get their work out there. If that is you, then this is one of many books that can help you on your way.

I have to stress there is no one answer that is applicable to all artists. Each artist has their own motive, their own way in to their work, where they want to go, what they want to do. It is always good to examine other points of view, even if only to solidify your own. As always, do what feels right to you. There are many books listed at the back of this book that might be helpful to you in various ways. It will never hurt to read and consider what they have to say and see if it applies or can help you.

Do your thing. Do it every day. Do it unapologetically. Don't be discouraged by criticism. You probably already know what they're going to say. Pay no mind to the fear of failure. It's far more valuable than success. Take ownership, take chances and have fun. And no matter what, don't ever stop doing your thing."
Asher Roth

Chapter 2 - Artists Today

Artists Today

The education level of the general populace of even pre-1950 was much lower than today. Our current public school system, while it has its faults, definitely has raised the bar of the median education and awareness. The people of days gone by didn't really have to worry much about saving the planet, or oil spills, but neither did they have the ability to instantly communicate with someone half way across the world in less time than it takes to walk to their bathroom. People lived in one room houses as opposed to four bedroom mansions.

We live with the ability to go off in comfort and have quiet space and time to ponder life, the universe and everything. With this education, this space to think also comes an increased ability to understand or project that understanding of possibility onto abstract concepts. With such an influx of information, and the ability to process it, the abstract is more commonly appreciated by Joe Public when it comes to everyday living.

At the same time however, there is so much information and technology coming in, and Joe Public is overwhelmed. He/she is looking to reconnect with their humanity, their ability to express, and have turned to the arts. It is a wonderful world of dichotomies that we live in.

As a result, some say (sometimes even me) that there doesn't seem to be many standards anymore. Outside that little box and sanctity of a museum or art gallery, anything goes. Everything is open game to be sold, all being prostitutes to the all mighty dollar.

But the economy is in terrible shape all around the world. People losing homes, funding cut to health care, essential services, doctors are needed, drug rehab centres are being closed down, the food banks are on the rise, non profits springing up to take up the slack and cuts in the social web.

The situation seems desperate to me. To survive in the present day as a professional artist requires new ways of thinking, and an acceptance that traditional methods of career progression are inadequate.

Contemporary Artists

Bill Moyers: Who interprets unseen things for us?

Joseph Campbell: It is the function of the artist to do this. The artist is the one who communicates myth for today. But he has to be an artist who understands mythology and humanity and isn't simply a sociologist with a program for you.[1]

The definition of the Contemporary Artist can be two fold. A Contemporary Artist is one who is living in society now, and who is reacting to that society. There is another definition of Contemporary Artist, which refers to someone who is acting "outside" of the normal artist expression. I am not qualified to say definitively which is the correct version, as I believe both are correct.

Regardless of their "style", artists are reactors and expressionists. The reasons they are highlighting troubles in our community by having their discourse on rocks, or on feminism, or oil spills, or such is because they are reacting to their environment. Other artists, whether they are doing pretty flowers, or Thomas Kinkade cottages, are reacting to their society, too. The reasons why they are expressing what they are require one to go deeper, as it is not as obvious as it may be assumed from the outside. Artists today concerned with environmental and social issues are just as important as those involved with fantasy worlds. It is how each sees or wishes to see their reality. If you are making art today, you are a Contemporary Artist.

Even in history many "contemporary" artists were questioned by the predominant representational and traditional artists on whether the art they created was, in fact, art. Questions regarding the subject, the style, the palette, and it goes on even now.[2] Context and/or the lack of, the understanding of their community impact, elevation of the public's education and knowledge, artists have contributed to where we are now.

---

1   Power of Myth, Joseph Campbell with Bill Moyers, Broadway Books, New York, 2001, p 99
2   But is it art? Cynthia Freeland, Oxford University Press, USA (April 4, 2002)

It is the artistic version of the H bomb where artists of yesterday, in their pursuit of awareness, pushed for the ever increasing lack of barriers to what is art. While the artists themselves, historical and contemporary, try to push the boundaries of what and where is art, it is Joe Public who are the ones really tearing them down. Everyone is an artist these days.

Many books have been written about this phenomena, with the focus on how to better access and develop the creative area of the brain. One of my favourite is by Julia Cameron, The Artist's Way[3] also listed in the Recommended Reading portion of this book. Not only will you discover worlds that are within yourself, but you will discover what drives you, what influences you and what prevents you from fulfilling your vision. In it you will learn about crazy makers, and how the biggest positive change you can give your business is also the hardest: limiting your exposure to these sorts of people.

Instant Gratification

Most people today live with the idea of instant gratification. They want things or knowledge now. I'll never be able to do what you outline in this book, they exclaim. Well, no, I answer. You aren't going to be able to do it all NOW, but you will be able to have it done in a year or two or three. Maybe this will be hard for you, maybe you will need to struggle a bit more than the next person. Don't be afraid to ask for help. If you never start working on the things you need to do, you will never get them done.

---

3   The Artist's Way, Julia Cameron, Tarcher; 10 Anv edition (March 4, 2002)

The Art World

It's all about connections and name recognition. Even though word of mouth is still the superior reference, you will still have to work hard. Success is 90% perspiration and 10% inspiration.[4] In that 90%, expect maybe 30-40% to be networking. Networking is hard. Authentic relationship building is harder and takes time.

Connections

If you have not read Seven Days in the Art World by Sarah Thornton, then do. It will give you a good idea of how everything works outside of the studio. [5]

Connections are the way, networking is hard work, and not comfortable for many of us introverted types. The only thing I can suggest is be yourself, be true to yourself, do not try to make yourself someone you are not. How much hot air you blow is entirely up to you. Some people have silver spoons, sure, it is a fact of life. Don't despair however, as you have control of how much hard work you put in to your career. You might have to do other jobs to pay the bills while you are working as an artist as well. These are connections too.

---

4   Thomas Alva Edison
5   Seven days in the art world, Sarah Thornton, WW Norton & Company, 2008

Chapter 3 - Why Are You an Artist?

Why Are You an Artist?

Questions to ask yourself include why are you an artist? What type of artist are you? Do you want to create just because you have to? Do you want to dedicate your life to creating art? What do you have to say? Why do you have to say it? How do you want to say it? What about living? How will you pay the bills or your student loan? These are questions that require answers, but recognize that the answers will change throughout your career as an artist. Priorities change. Life experience is flux, allow it to change, and you will have a joyful time.

As an example, here are some of my answers:

Because it is a way to communicate beyond words. Because it is my goal to learn about the human experience, through my own and relate to others, to create worlds where we live, and I believe we live in more than one. It is to accept ourselves including our faults. It is to understand and convey we don't have to be perfect to be loved or accepted, because I believe truly that we are not alone, even though we sometimes live lonely lives. Because even though we are separate beings, I believe that an experience I have, is shared and understood by many others. Because I believe that we have no other option but to connect to each other, whether emotionally, mentally or spiritually.

An artist is someone who uses bravery, insight, creativity, and boldness to challenge the status quo. And an artist takes it personally. That's why Bob Dylan is an artist, but an anonymous corporate hack who dreams up Pop 40 hits on the other side of the glass is merely a marketer.
Seth Godin

I create art to discover my own truth, to get at the grass roots - the authenticity of existence. I am not out to shock the world, or to shock my neighbours or create works that please others or follow a fad. I don't use schticks, but change my style as the expression requires.

I create work that pleases me - and by doing so, understand myself, and, as a consequence, my surroundings which includes other people. My goal is not to be the best artist or the most famous artist, or the richest artist; my goal is to be an honest artist, an adventurer, with the courage to speak my truth. I can guarantee that you resonate with some, if not all of the above.

Artists Today are Multi-Dimensional Beings

"Man is his own star; and the soul that can
Render an honest and a perfect man,
Commands all light, all influence, all fate;
Nothing to him falls early or too late.
Our acts our angels are, or good or ill,
Our fatal shadows that walk by us still."
John Fletcher, Epilogue to Beaumont and Fletcher's Honest Man's Fortune

The art world requires you to be a business person too, and know what your work is about. You also should know why you are an artist.

I am fairly certain the perception of the general public is that we artists don't really do much except paint and dream and don't really work hard. Ever had someone talk to you about their "real" job? And what the hell does thinking have to do with making art?

The artists of my generation were not always artists. Without revealing my age, and thinking too hard, I know many people who are currently practicing artists but who had a traditional working job prior to committing to being a full time artist.

Previous careers indicate we possess a diverse multi dimensional experience. These careers indicate an aptitude for organization (all right, maybe not always), initiative, sometimes intuition but most definitely intelligence. Use this knowledge, make it work for you in your current artistic career. All this previous experience informs your work. It has to. And it makes it and you, incredibly rich and unique.

16

Self Reliance

Everything you have done before is important to making art now.

If you have not read Sir Ralph Waldo Emerson's Self-Reliance, you can do so here. http://www.emersoncentral.com/essays1.htm[1]

While this text was written in 1841, the ideas and attitudes he puts forth are as applicable today as they were back then. It talks about taking charge of your life, and your actions. It talks about not blaming others for what happens to you. It talks about not being the victim anymore. Are you ready for this ....?

I'll start you off ....

"I read the other day some verses written by an eminent painter which were original and not conventional. The soul always hears an admonition in such lines, let the subject be what it may. The sentiment they instill is of more value than any thought they may contain. To believe your own thought, to believe that what is true for you in your private heart is true for all men, — that is genius. ...."

Later on in the essay he gets a bit preachy, in my humble opinion, but is still worth reading. I have read it over and over again, especially when I am feeling down or not in control.

---

1   http://www.emersoncentral.com/essays1.htm

Education vs Self-Taught

Is a Fine Arts degree required to be a professional artist? No. Having said that however, I do believe that having a background in Art History, and the Fundamentals of Art, is important. For those who are just starting out, by Art History I believe it is important to study those artists who have had an impact on the world. And when I say study them, I mean study their art, but also why they had such an impact on society. What made them stand out? I believe it is as valuable to study the ones you like, but more importantly, to study the ones you don't like. See as much art in person as you can - local art shows, museums, galleries and if you are able, abroad. I am a fan of art history. I love it. It is validating and enlightening.

By Fundamentals, I mean the five main ones - Line, Value, Shape, Texture, Colour and also the ideas of composition. The Golden Rule. Other rules, [2] Learn them, then break them.

One thing you will also find in studying the history and the fundamentals, is that if you can think it, you can do it. Maybe others have done it before, that's okay.[3] Some people think that it has all already been done. That's okay too. Authentic art does not come from the outside, but from the inside. The only permission you need to give is to yourself.

I've encountered three types of people. The first two are ego based: immediately upon meeting them, I am told, I come from XX school (therefore I must be good) or I am self taught (therefore I must be a savant). I understand that these first two are coming from a space of insecurity, where they feel the need to justify their artwork based on their background, so I just try to smile and nod. The third type are the ones I admire the most. They are the ones who don't really say much at all about their background, but let the work speak for them.

---

2   Art Fundamentals: Theory and Practice by Robert E. Stinson, Philip R. Wigg, Robert O. Bone and David L.. Cayton, Mcgraw-Hill College; 8th edition (August 6, 1997)
3   Steal like an Artist, Austin Kleon, Workman Publishing Company; First Edition edition (February 28, 2012)

I can not help to say though that stating one is self taught, is a misnomer, because all artists are really self taught. The majority of technical application is learned outside of the educational institution, as their focus of study is that of the concept or the idea. One can say self taught to differentiate between those who have the letters behind their name, to be sure - but truly, one is not better than the other. It's all identity, and what you identify with.

"Academic qualifications are absolutely no measure of intelligence, but that's what the system demands because examination passes confirm that you have passed successfully through its indoctrination machine."
David Icke

Why get a BFA or an MFA or such? Some people are interested in the academics. Some people need the structure, some like being in the educational arena, some want the initials. Some need the initials depending on the path that they wish their art career to take. Some need the connections that come from a university settings. These are all valid depending on the goals of that artist.

Specific Schools?

We, as a society, have gotten caught up in getting the right brands, the right contacts, the right friends, and it's draining our souls and our pocketbooks. Rather than the inwardly supported affirmation of our own preferences, we rely instead on being told what is good. I think this attitude is changing. The school can give you only so much, it is what you do with your skills that will matter.

Again, I believe the quality of art work is not because of the school the artist went to, but from the quality of character it comes from. Don't get hung up on the idea that you didn't go to the "right" school.

To Sell or Not to Sell

Do you want to sell your work? Or are you one of these people who say "I'm just doing it for the expression, the joy, the heart, the soul"? Most professional artists I know do it for those reasons, but the difference is that they are committed to their work, they believe in their work.

Have you gone through the "oh, your work really speaks to me"? I've given work away because I was so touched that they would tell me that. After encountering individuals who use this to get free art, and to take advantage of the artist by also asking "is this your best price?" After the third or fourth time, this no longer works on me. Don't let it work on you.

Professional vs Unprofessional

The government's definition of a professional artist is one who works full time as an artist, and who derives the majority of their income from their artwork.

The Canada Council for the Arts, the non profit entity that governs the disbursement of funds to professional artists and other cultural persons, defines a professional artist as:

A professional artist is someone who:

1. has specialized training in the field (not necessarily in academic institutions),
2. is recognized as such by peers (artists working in the same artistic tradition), and
3. has a history of public presentation or publication.

In the community, an artist who is not full time can still be a popular artist, sell their work, develop an excellent reputation. Reputation also factors into the price one is able to put on their work.

Reputation and Community Work

Reputation can be in the community, in teaching, in volunteer work, etc. I truly believe that community work is a must for the artist, professional or not. It is character development. Volunteer on a board, or help out at the local animal shelter, or foster kittens, or work an hour a week at the Hospice, or something!

The reason I am saying this is because it will help you get to know your community more, it will keep one foot grounded in reality when you are off lost in your world of charcoal, paint or stone. It will connect you with people who care about the same things you do, and you will make genuine acquaintances and friends outside the art world. I am not talking about what can be the fabricated networking done at social events where everyone is nice to your face, but talks behind your back. I am talking about salt of the earth, genuine heart to heart people.

Professional Artist

Remember, when I refer to a professional artist, I am talking about either one or two things - that they derive the majority of their income from their artwork, or they have the reputation of being a professional artist.

WIth today's economy, I find it very hard to believe that there are many artists out there making a living solely from their art. I am pretty sure most are supplementing their income with other jobs or projects. And that's okay. Do what you need to do.

Self employed vs Employee

As a professional artist, you may encounter times where you are on commission, or contract, or are in fact employed as an artist. Go to the Canada Revenue Agency website: http://www.cra-arc.gc.ca/E/pub/tp/it504r2-consolid/it504r2-consolid-e.html for the up to date information.

The basic premise is, do you have control over your work practices? If yes, you are self employed.

Not a Professional Artist

When I refer to an artist who is not professional, it means that they do not have a reputation, nor do they sell their artworks. They are just entering school, just finishing school, just bought their new box of paints, have been painting for a hundred years on Sundays. They are 8 years old, or 89 years old. They have not yet said, okay, I'm committed as an artist and I'm going to get out there. They have not done the work or put in the time to create that reputation or done schooling (which can include hands-on workshops) to further their technical or academic knowledge.

Ask Yourself This Question, and It's an Important One

Are you a professional artist or not?

A lot of people think they are professional artists these days. Everyone can draw, it is just hand eye dexterity after all. Everyone can paint, everyone can sing, everyone can act - the difference is what is your commitment to your ability? What do you do with that ability, how do you use it and do you respect your talents?

What this whole discourse was about was to help you decide if you haven't already, if you are professional, or aren't, and to determine your investment of time and energy in your career. This chapter was more focussed on someone who has not yet made that decision, what's involved, some viewpoints and questions they should ask themselves.

Be Flexible

Regardless if you are a professional artist or not, always be flexible and open to change. Nothing is ever constant, not in your work, not in your life, and not in your career. Be adaptable and go with the flow. You will be much happier, guaranteed.

What Are Your Intentions?

Is your intention to make the majority of your income from your art? Are you registered with the government? Do you have a business name? This is usually your own or it could be like a mini statement about your work. Do you have a business license? Do you spend the majority of your time on your art? Do you give your artwork the respect and honour it deserves as a creation from your heart, mind, body and soul? Have you committed to your work? Have you dedicated time or been hired on to be a Commercial Artist? Do you have a specific place for your work where you can go to create - (it could be something as informal as a corner in the dining room, or an unused bedroom etc)? Do you have a firm price structure? Do you deserve the prices you put on your work, or do you just give most of it away anyway? Do you have a map?

Chapter 4 - Do You Have a Map?

Do You Have a Map?

A map is a one year goal, five year or even ten year goal that lists your tools, your assets, and your compass. It also known more commonly as a Business Plan, but artists I've talked to freak out when I say Business Plan, but are okay with the idea of a map. It's all semantics, but use whatever term works for you.

Whether you are a professional artist, or whether you have a traditional job, or career, you will need a map, a plan for moving forward in your life. It's hard work, and takes time to think but dedicating time to this part of your career will pay off in the long run.

Being a professional artist can be just as much a business - you still have expenses, you still have to produce work, regardless if it sells or not.

You, as an artist, are always continually evolving, continually growing. It is your personality, your point of view, your existence that you use as fodder for your artworks, whether you sell or not.

What is on Your Map?

Yourself
Your artwork
Places for your artwork
People in your world
Compass
Method of travel
Time line/time table
Evaluation criteria
Other tools you may need

Yourself, Who Are You?

Where are you in this whole realm? Where is your starting point? Where do you want to go? It helps to know why you are where you are. It helps to know your values. Take a Myers Briggs or Keirsey test if you haven't done that already.[1]

---

1   http://www.myersbriggs.org or http://www.keirsey.com

Who you are can be discovered through the paper toolbox which includes your biography, and your Curriculum Vitae (CV) as well as your artist statement and titles. More on that later.

Your Artwork

Pretty self explanatory, but if you do different styles, or different mediums, your artwork may have different destinations or ability to be seen. Consider your titles and artist statements as part of who you are. Your artwork also includes prices: the starting point, and time built in for the raising of prices as your work becomes known and desired.

Places for Your Artwork

Where do you put your work? Physically, this would include public galleries, commercial galleries, artist run galleries, coffee shops, restaurants, offices, etc. On the web, this would include websites, blogs, Facebook, Google+, Pinterest etc.

People in Your World

People in your world include family, friends and other cheerleaders such as other artists, and the media. More on the People in your world in another chapter called Cheerleaders.

Method of Travel

This can include education, books and other knowledge stuff. It can be investment in the community and resulting relationships that go back to the people in your world. It is any method that moves your artwork in to the public sphere such as shows, galleries, the internet and email, and newsletters.

Time Line/Time Table

What is your time line? Where do you want to be in one year? In five years? In ten years? Be imaginative, and dream. Pretend nothing is too big to obtain. Write it down and don't worry about the how just yet. In your time line, have areas built in for re-evaluation as well. Maybe a project that you thought would be important five years from now is no longer relevant. Be realistic and flexible.

Maybe you're the type of person who likes to fly by the seat of your pants, or be footloose and fancy free and can not be troubled to do a timeline, or plan for the future. I'd wager too that you would have trouble meeting deadlines, whether self imposed or not. Maybe it works for you. You should skip this section then, and maybe even the whole book.

Below is the project timeline for this book:

Item	Goal	Timeline	Item	Complete
1	One year	Nov 12-13	Book A&M	Yes
1.a.	Checkpoint	May 2013	Draft	Yes
1.b.	Checkpoint	Jul 2013	Submit to Pub	Yes
1.c.	Re-eval	Sep 2013	Adjustments?	Yes

Compass

This is constantly changing as you move forward. Keeping your eyes on your goals, you put in to action your plans. It means that you have to keep yourself objective to the future, while acting out in the present. It means deciding maybe to not do a specific project if it will take you too far off track. It means looking at your goals and deciding which to action, where you will do it, making the time and space commitment to see the goal through.

Making a Timeline

Do you know how to make a timeline for your projects? Many people actually do not and think it is very complicated. It's pretty simple.

Take the farthest deadline, i.e. when you want something accomplished, and then move backwards, putting in to place how long each step will take you. If, for example, you have a show, and your goal is to have twenty artworks by the end of nine months, consider how long one artwork will take you. Be generous with yourself - if a step such as creating an artwork will take you three weeks to accomplish, then add a buffer of one week perhaps. That means that twenty artworks will take you twenty months. This means that you need to do some adjusting to meet your goal, whether it is the number of artworks, the time it takes to do an artwork, or if you have that flexibility, the end date itself.

Example, artwork based:
It is January 20th, and you have a deadline of September 10th for twenty artworks. You have to buy supplies, and also do research on your subject. Perhaps you are already somewhat familiar with your subject, and the research will only take a week or two, you are sure.

You know from past experience that you can work on two or three artworks at most, at the same time. The supplies you have to buy are from the local store, but it is always a good three hour venture from start to when you get back home. This is accounting for traffic and also customers at the store in front of you.

When I do planning, I account for every hour I can think of, to be the most efficient at time expenditure. After I am done my time planning, I add a few hours (or days depending on the project) to include Murphy. I find inviting him to my project always makes my life easier.

Timeline for an Art Project

I make notes such as the following:

Start: January 20
End: September 10
Goal: 20 artworks but 10 artworks minimum needed for the show

Stuff to do:
- buy supplies 4 hours (3 hours plus an hour adjustment)
- prep surfaces

2-3 artworks at a time
General expectation, 3 artworks a month.

Checkpoint	Action/work completed	Artworks underway
Jan 20	Buy supplies	
Jan 25	Prep artwork	.5
Feb 1	.5	1.5
Mar 1	3	3
Apr 1	5	4
May 1	9	3

From this timeline, you can see that by Sep 10, I will probably have around the 20 artworks completed. Because I inflate the final goal, which means I always plan for more than I need, I will be able to choose the minimum ten works that I like the best for the show.

You can make a timeline for your map in the same manner as you would for an art project. Just list out your variables, and plug in the times. Always plan for requiring more time than you actually need.

Other Tools You May Need

Invest time in the back end skill of bookkeeping, as well as how to do your taxes I would suggest taking classes from the local college or university once you feel interested enough to learn.

For me, I use a program called QuickTax, which is put out by Intuit who also provides a software called QuickBooks. I would recommend getting both of these, as they make the job of doing your bookkeeping and taxes much easier. (No, I am not getting a commission for the endorsement.)

Programs I use to edit my artwork or to do posters or such include Photoshop and Illustrator. To write this book, I am using InDesign. To do my webpage/blog, I use an independent installation of WordPress. To bulk upload files to my website, I use Filezilla.

If you were to invest in one program, get a graphics program like Photoshop - make sure you can do the editing features such as cropping, light adjustment, colour adjustment and size adjustment. Take a class. It's definitely worth the time investment. That's all you really need. The rest of the non-Adobe programs mentioned are free versions though I do "donate" to the developers for their use. It is their hard work that makes mine easier.

Outcomes & Evaluations

I always do an evaluation on the results of anything I do. Was it successful? Will it be worth repeating again? What went well and what could be better (the standard WWW and WCBB you will find in any business event). Results can be personal, social, environmental, economic, and they can be present initially, immediately or be present in the long term or in the future. Be on the look out for those unexpected results as well, they should never be underestimated. Those are the wild cards you never know where they will lead.

Chapter 5 - The Paper Toolbox

The Paper Toolbox

Artists today must have five things, not counting the art, in their toolbox for deployment on their map:

1. Biographies
2. Curriculum Vitae (CV)
3. Titles
4. Artist Statements
5. Inventory tracking

Biographies, CVs, titles and artist statements have structures surrounding them.

Biographies

Note that it is biography, not an auto biography. A biography is told third person while an auto-biography is first person. Photographs of the art will be talked about in its own section of this book.

Where I was born and where and how I have lived is unimportant. It is what I have done with where I have been that should be of interest.
Georgia O'Keeffe

One day your life will flash before your eyes.
Make sure it is worth watching.
Gerard Way

Make sure your biography is worth reading.

Your Reader's Attention Span

Think about your reader's attention span. In a nutshell, you need three types:

1. One liner: make it short and snappy, a one liner that you can throw out there to give a quick snapshot but that will generate interest - this is especially useful as a meta description for your artist biography web page.

2. Short: One paragraph that you can use in promo and print, usually about 100 words, and

3. Long: Two or three paragraphs that you can use when submitting articles, artworks, or where you need something that tells a little bit of your life story, no more than 500 words.

You now have the structure of what you need to write, you just need the content.

Make a list of facts from your life, such as given below, and then ask a friend to write it for you. Do NOT say you've been drawing or painting since you were two, four or six, or a child or your teens. DO include what made you do the "C" word - "commit" to being an artist.

Do some research on other artists what information they include in their biographies. Look up local artists, artists the same age as you, artists who are older, artists who are dead. Analyze their biographies. Why did they include certain things and why are these important? Relate these findings to your own life. No one else has your story so be proud to write it.

Curriculum Vitae (CV)

CVs are also known as the artist resume. It tells the gallery owner, Executive Director, Curator who you are in terms of commitment and recognition of you and your work.

You will have two main versions of these. The first one is the complete CV and can be endless. List everything you have done in your life, as an artist and otherwise. The second one will be the short CV, one to three pages, where you choose what you will include, depending on the situation, i.e. applying for an exhibition, a grant, a residency etc.

Sub-headings for your complete CV will include items such as:

1. Your name, address and contact information including email and phone.
2. Education
3. Exhibitions: Solo and Group
4. Honours & Awards
5. Collections - Public & Private
6. Professional Experience - Artist
7. Professional Experience - Administrative
8. Professional Experience - Financial
9. Published (books your work is in, writer or artist)
10. Professional Affiliations (such as Art Galleries and other groups)

This complete CV will also list your abilities and experience in other jobs or careers that you have. List your administrative abilities, typing, all of what you can do. When you go to apply for a traditional job, perhaps in an art gallery or a museum, you don't have to stress over it, you can just pluck out what you do need, create a mini targeted CV, and add the goal line at the top (i.e. Goal: To do, to obtain, to further, to expand etc). The all encompassing CV can be endless, 20 pages, 30 pages even more. This one is seldom given out intact. Keep it updated as you accomplish projects and it will make your life so much easier.

If you find your CV is lacking in one or more areas, choose an area and focus on filling that gap. It could be collections, exhibitions, etc but focus on having an entry under that heading.

Short CV

The short CV does not have to include all the headings from your main CV. It is short and targeted. It contains pertinent information to the situation you are creating it for. It is one to three pages in length.

Perhaps your short CV will only include the Education, Exhibitions, and Honours and Awards section. Even in these sections, be choosy about what you will include. Think about what will make the most impact on your target audience. Do not make things up, do not exaggerate. This is not the time for creative thinking.

The order in which you arrange your CV will depend on what item is the most noteworthy. If you are newly out of school, and have no real exhibitions, then list your education first. If you have been awarded a major exhibition at a public art gallery, perhaps you will list your exhibitions first. If you have an artwork in a major collection, then perhaps have your Collections list first.

Organization

When I update my main complete CV, I always rename the file with the date I added information, i.e. MainCVJan2013 and I do not delete the old file. I have my current CV on my website in case of interest from clients or galleries.

When I do create any CVs for specific reasons, then I save them in my computer under the folder cv & bio as a specific title, i.e. MiniCV Admin Jan2013 or MiniCV Fin Jan2013. When I go apply for a similar job, they are nice and handy to adjust quickly and simply.

Titles

I used to be a proponent of leaving my artworks untitled - but now I think that is a big mistake, and a missed opportunity.

The philosophy of the unnamed artwork remaining the undiscovered, unbiased potential available for each viewer does have merit. It does provide an open door for the person viewing the artwork to make their own judgements, their own opinions. It does detach the artist from the artwork, so that it can stand alone. It allows the viewer to focus on the surface, the methods of creation, the formal elements such as composition and rhythm. But after that, then what? Maybe that is enough?

Naming an artwork is a lot of work on the part of the artist. It is a big responsibility and it requires the artist to be vulnerable.

Usually, people will see the artwork from far away, and be introduced to its colours, its composition, the vibe. Something will have caught their eye, and make them curious. After a person approaches an artwork, they will either look at it some more, walk closer, or walk farther to see it at a distance, or they might stoop to see the writing on the card.

I like watching people to see what they do - it is a curiosity of mine, to consider if they are right-brained or left-brained. Right-brained will like to explore the work first. Left-brained people want the facts. Neither is wrong, it is just interesting to see the approaches. You can use the way the person approaches the artwork (or even approaches you with questions about the artwork) in any subsequent conversations about the work: left-brained people want to know about facts, and stats whereas right-brained people want to know about emotions, feelings. Respond to them in-kind.

I look at naming the artwork as an opportunity to provide a mini artist statement, a way for the person to connect to the artwork through words. The naming of an artwork provides a whole other dimension for the viewer, and sometimes even the artist, to explore. The title helps to consolidate their thoughts, or introduce new ones. Naming an artwork can be scary, and it can be tremendous fun.

Titles can indicate methods, or maybe it is part of a series, or an example of a smaller concept inside the whole. Maybe there is some other esoteric reason for the title. Maybe it was the music being listened to while it was created. Maybe the title is exactly what the artwork is "House on a Hill". The title can be a strong indication what the philosophy of the artist is without being directly expressed. It can be implied with the structure of the words.

The whole reason for the existence of art is to express and communicate, and to communicate effectively, I think you have to try to reach more levels of understanding or awareness. If your goal or your inclination is to be exclusionary, and only appeal to a select group of individuals, then be reclusive and elusive. Do you want your work to have staying power, or when another Abstract Red #3 comes in will they remember yours?

Titles are hard work. But worth it. Think of the worlds you would be opening up for someone, and for yourself.

Artist Statements

You need one, period. Get over your reluctance to write it. It's tough to do, yes. But it's expected, and the professional artist has one (or more).

I had always firmly avoided doing an artist statement, and while I do understand that the artist statement in itself is a method of education, I had always been turned off by those who write statements that require the average person a dictionary in order to read it, and the worst thing an artist can do is to talk down or alienate the viewer. Is it about the artwork or is it about who can read ten letter words?

"Artists must assume the responsibility for education of their dealers and collectors by speaking intelligently about their own work."
Sylvia White

Speaking intelligently includes stating the reasons why you are painting what you are painting, if they are known, or your influences, why they are your influences. Understand art history, so you can understand where you are in the current art scene, whether local, regional, or global. Write and write and write. If you can't write, then find someone who will help you. You should expect to pay them, unless you can work out a trading agreement. Writers (and photographers) are creative people too, and if it is hard for you to write or photograph, then remember you should pay them for their abilities, just as you expect to be paid for yours.

The only other thing I can say about Artist Statements, is I don't believe you should tell the viewer what they should be seeing or feeling. If there is something that you feel, then identify as such, not that the viewer should feel it. In personal interactions, have that one liner artist statement available and ready to be the segue between the title and you, the artist, to facilitate discussion of the work.

The Inventory

Track your inventory. Keep a list of what artworks you make, how long it takes to make them, when they sell, where they go, who they go to (if you can), add the client's email to your newsletter list. This will help in your analysis of what works and what doesn't. Your inventory can be a book, or it can be a spreadsheet in Excel, it is up to you. Yes, it's a pain in the ass, and I dislike doing it too, but do it anyway.

Summary

It may feel like an overwhelming amount of work that you have to do, if you don't have this done already. It can be, no doubt about it. Set aside some time to start with one thing, maybe it will be the CV. Start by listing everything you have done in your life, do this for maybe half an hour. Perhaps the next day, go back and highlight items, giving them colour codes to make the organization easier. Sort items out to the headings. As you see your past actions materialize, maybe then the biography will flow a bit better. But start. That's the hardest part, is to start. Take a deep breath and take the plunge.

"People do not care how much you know
until they know how much you care."
John Maxwell

Chapter 6 - Galleries

Galleries

Before we talk about prices, we need to deal with where you are selling. This section will deal with the physical space of showing work, which is in a gallery. Where you sell your work will have an impact on the price you put on it, and sometimes too, what type of work you sell can make a difference as well.

There are two types of galleries: non profit and commercial. Non profit includes the local public art gallery, and the artist run galleries. Commercial galleries are the regular galleries who select artists and show/sell their work. Vanity Galleries will show anyone (pretty much) who can pay their fees.

Non Profit Public Art Galleries

Non Profit Public Art Galleries seldom sell work. Shows in a non profit Public Art Gallery are usually project based, or based on a premise or an idea of the Curator employed by that gallery. The Public Art Gallery shows artists they deem worthy or interesting to the general public, based on their mission statement established by their Board of Directors, and based on the fulfilment of requirements of their major financial sponsors. A show in a Public Art Gallery can increase the value of that artist's work.

Non Profit Artist Run Galleries

Artist Run Galleries usually have the principle of showing work that is perceived to be intellectually challenging to other artists. Similar to the Public Art Galleries, they also have a mandate established by a Board of Directors. Artist Run Galleries usually have a yearly membership fee attached to them. If work is available for sale, and it sells, there is a commission to the gallery to help pay for costs.

Volunteering at an Artist Run Gallery can be enlightening and profitable, in more ways than relating to money, so consider doing that. It might be uncomfortable at first, but these are the pains of growth. Welcome them.

Commercial Galleries

Commercial galleries look at their available wall space in terms of real estate, as that is their way of generating money. Financially, they consider how much space they have, how much that space is worth, and they try to provide their clientele with work that would interest them. Their goal is to sell art. Their fees are back end, and paid when the work sells.

Many times commercial galleries will find you based on group shows that you do, or if you are in a nearby coffee shop or restaurant. They might find you because of statements in your blog, or your work with the community, or from a newspaper article, or a radio show.

Do research to find out a good gallery match, then submit according to their requirements as detailed on their web site. For heaven sake don't write them to ask something that would have been easily found with a bit of searching on your part.

If there is one thing I personally can not stand it is a lazy artist.

One day I may have a gallery of my own, and I can tell you that any artist who writes me to ask a question that is easily found in my FAQ page will not even receive an answer. So do your research. Be thorough. Look at their artists. Look at their focus. If they already have someone doing the same style of work that you are doing, then maybe that isn't the gallery for you. Do your work and then do your homework.

Galleries are great places to sell your work. Normally they are run by people of education and knowledge. Do your research on the gallery owners. Who are they? What are their interests? What is their history and what does their future look like? Write to one you are interested in, and ask them questions about these things. If it were me as the gallery owner, I would appreciate it, because it would show me you would be an active participant in the success of my gallery.

Be prepared though, in these times, that the galleries may not be accepting new artists unless your work is very unique, or you come with your own set of patrons. Galleries are hurting just as much as any other business these days, they have to pay overhead the same as anyone else. If you do not get accepted to the galleries you were hoping, keep looking, keep applying.

Documentation

There are standards of conduct expected of both you and them. Once you are in, first and primarily, document all interaction with them. Have a written record of what works are in the galleries. Sign and date the consignment form. If the gallery goes out of business, this is the only way you will get your artwork back. A little bit of forethought and planning will save you tons of headaches in the future. I believe that preparing for problems facilitates the solutions.

Exclusivity Clause

If a gallery asks you to sign an Exclusivity clause, it means that you agree to not sell your work on your own, or with anyone else, or anywhere within the boundaries of that Exclusivity Clause. It is a restriction the gallery requests so that anyone in that geographic area interested in your work goes to them, as they would be the experts in your work in that area. I think that is very understandable. You may also be required to obtain their permission to show outside the gallery. I think this is pretty understandable as well, as there are business decisions made regarding artist profiling, prices and such. If you do show outside of the gallery in a group show for example, it would make sense that the sales go through them.

In a Gallery But Selling Work Outside the Gallery

If you have work in the gallery and you have an agreement with them that they are to be your representative in a certain area then make sure you honour that agreement. That means that any works you sell on your own, you still need to give commission to the gallery for those works.

Perhaps you have a few artworks in a commercial gallery and someone comes to you and says hey, I'd like to buy a work from you. For sure, sell, but still give the gallery their commission. Artists and galleries are honour bound to treat each other fairly.

Under no circumstances should you be selling artworks behind the gallery's back and not giving them their commission, or for less and not giving commission. That is wrong. It is called undercutting the gallery. Nothing ever stays hidden, people talk, and once it is found out that you dishonoured the gallery, they may terminate their agreement to represent you. You may not care, but you will care when you find out that galleries talk to each other, and they talk to artists too. It's just not worth it.

Vanity Galleries

Vanity Galleries are those who want you to pay a fee for displaying art - I call them "Pay to Play". Note, the fee is for displaying art only, and there is no guarantee of selling. You are renting their wall space only. In addition to the fee you are charged for display, there is also a commission.

Do I think these are legitimate for a gallery? Sure, it's a legitimate business for them. All the costs are borne by the artist, and there is no risk for the Vanity Gallery. These galleries usually are in high traffic areas and market themselves as advantageous for being seen. In my opinion, it is a business that literally makes a living off of the back of an artist. I don't like them.

Due to the economic collapse, not many people are buying art these days as it isn't really high on the list and many galleries are suffering because of it. But "pay to play" - I don't know. To say you've shown in New York, to Joe Public it might mean something on your CV, but to those knowledgeable about the galleries, it could hurt more than it could help.

Summary

Galleries have overhead, they advertise, they put on shows, they put a lot of work and investment in the artist and selling one's art and I believe they earn their commission. On principle, and for strictly financial reasons, I would stay away from Vanity Galleries, but not Artist Run Galleries. Do your research so you know the difference for your area.

I would also keep an eye on your future, and not discount showing in the non profit art galleries, whether public or artist run. It would be a good challenge for you to have your works in different intellectual spheres and those resulting interactions, no matter how uncomfortable.

Chapter 7 - The Marketplace

The Marketplace

Before determining your prices, questions you need to ask are:

Where are you in the marketplace?
Are you marketing?
What marketing materials do I need?
Are you doing potstickers?
Are you selling local?
If you are selling local, where are you selling?
Who are your audience/clients?
How much art are you donating?
Are you selling on the internet?
Are you selling in galleries locally or abroad?
What are other ways to raise money?

The philosophy surrounding the above are pretty much the same, which is **prices must be consistent.** Decisions need to be made. The internet is a big place, and the competition out there is much fiercer than it might be locally or regionally.

Where Are You in the Market Place?

Research your town. Research on the internet. Find the artists who are doing similar subjects, similar styles, similar mediums. What is their background? How long have they been practicing? How long have they been selling? What are their prices? You can not reasonably expect to enter the marketplace with top dollar prices for your work. It is much like a young person thinking they are entitled to start off as CEO for their very first job. You still have to do the time, pay your dues. It is said that it is easy for prices to go up, but hard for them to come down. Prices are dealt with in another section of this book.

When marketers talk about marketing, they discuss the concept of brands, and identifiers. In art, you are the brand. Remember that your brand is a verb, not a noun. It is not a logo. It is what you stand for and it is your name.

Are You Marketing?

Here is what I do. If I am doing something, I say so. If I am involved with other groups, I say so. If I am involved in your group, it is because I believe in it, and/or I am proud of it. I wouldn't be hanging out with you if you didn't have something positive to offer the community. I wouldn't be hanging out with you if I didn't have something positive to offer YOU! These days it seems it is really hard to get people involved in outside artist activities... So be happy that anyone is involved in your project, whether it is me, or Joe the Plumber! Be happy that I'm blabbing (or blogging) about it! You should be too. And if you aren't, why aren't you?

Is this really marketing? Sure. You as an artist, are a brand. Any time you open your mouth to say what you are doing, you are marketing. For example, even when I am not marketing my art, if I am doing a unrelated activity, I am still marketing my art, because I am known as an artist. The art is seldom separated from the artist, how can it be, really, when you think about it. The art is a reflection of what is inside of you, you are a walking advertisement for your work. So walk tall! Remember, you, as a brand, are a verb not a noun.

Eighty percent of marketing is being strong enough to stand up and say something out loud to many people who may or may not be listening. It doesn't really matter if they are listening, it matters that you are standing up and saying it. People are going to remember your name because they either:

1. really love your artwork, or
2. really hate it, or
3. can't believe that you are telling others about it, or
4. because they can't believe you're such an unrealistic dreamer.

All of the above are completely acceptable, because they are going to remember your name.

Marketing Materials

I use a printing service called Vistaprint, which is available all over the world, and the quality is usually pretty good. Depending on what you want, the price can not be beat by local printing companies. They are reliable, definitely. I've used them for almost five years now for business cards and postcards, though I get posters and such printed at the local Staples. You already have your paper toolbox done. After you've got your images done, your next step is to create some marketing materials such as business cards, postcards to send to galleries or to give out at your next show or at your studio.

Are You Doing Potstickers?

Potstickers are those artworks that bring in funds. Potstickers can be any size. They may be smaller work, larger works, they may be prints, they may be something that is not your normal line of work. They are fast and easy to do, they are accessible price-wise by Joe Public, both locally and on the internet, they may follow fads, you may even create the fad for them, and they allow your name to get out there. They generate funds. That is their only purpose.

Are You Selling Locally?

Do your research on local artists. Where are they selling? Some ideas might be coffee shops, bars, restaurants, public spaces, libraries, wander around town, and look to see what is on the walls, what type of artworks. Are they originals or prints? What does your doctor's office have, or your lawyer, or accountant, or dentist .... you get the idea. Ask them if they would consider putting your work up on their walls to sell. Remember you are doing them a favour and elevating their business personae by involving the cultural aspect of original art, make them feel involved, help them believe in you. You are patronizing their business because you believe in them, right? You also might consider entering in to a "rent-to-own" contract with them, or barter for services.

Who Is Your Audience and What Do They Want?

Where I am in Okanagan, it is a very different kind of marketplace. We are a resort town during the summer and a retiree town for the majority of the remainder of the year. There are a multitude of other reasons that I will get in to later, but it is mostly the seniors who really have no need or desire to buy artwork or it's the younger group, or younger families who don't have a lot of disposable income who live here year round. It's a tough world out there right now.

I've sold well over a thousand works just on the internet and one day, just for fun, my husband and I put a dot where each artwork went over the past fifteen years just to see how much was local and how much was not. Locally my sales were about 5% of my total sales. It was a very useful exercise regarding location and really made the value of the internet clear to me. Because of the internet, my work has gone to the eastern States primarily, New York down along the coast and over to Georgia and Florida, then to Alabama, Texas and California. Through conversations with my clients, I have discovered that my demographic is 35-65 females, who are usually professionals. These are women who are doing their own self discovery and self analysis. I am sure a book could be written just on this subject, but the implications were clear.

One Small Step

If you are selling local, it is one small step to sell on the internet. One word of advice though, keep your prices the same. Decide if you plan on doing prints. Some websites such as RubyLane where I presently sell my work do not permit prints, while others facilitate them, such as Etsy, or FineArtAmerica.

Look at the prices on each of these sites as well - prices for original art on Etsy is less than RubyLane. Prices for prints are less on Etsy than FineArtAmerica. Again, do your homework, and find your place. You do have one. There is room for all.

Originals vs Prints

It's really a philosophical question. When I refer to prints, it is always to the mechanical sort, not to original prints such as lithos (real lithos), intaglios or real silk screens. Some mechanical prints are done on the home computer, some are done in a print shop, but they are all done from a mechanical process.

While I do not do prints as that is my philosophy, there are many artists who do. This might be their method of potstickers, doing prints of their work on paper, canvas, coffee mugs, shopping bags, shoes and even iPhone cases and such. These are all valid methods of raising funds. Robert Bateman and Thomas Kinkade made a whole pile of money from prints, making editions of their work in the tens of hundreds of thousands.

Artists in our art history, and by history I mean prior to 1900, never had to deal with multiples of their work being thrust in to the public sphere. Maybe it is because there weren't a lot of people who could afford even the prints - or maybe they would have been, if the printing services had been available. Begs an interesting question doesn't it? I think that those pre-1900 artists had enough to deal with in breaking the representational and the traditional painting rules, than have to contend with issues of reproduction that we have today.

I often have received questions about whether to do prints of work, or not. My answer is this:

I can tell you unabashedly that I am not a fan of mechanical prints, and quite bluntly, I believe that artists who do prints bring down the value of their work. Some people will not agree, that is their prerogative. For me, I will not do prints of my work. I believe that part of my role as an artist is to help people understand the value of original work - yes, you pay for it, but there is a reason it is costly - it is the only one.

If you were to do prints, you need to justify it within yourself, without regard to what other people think. Do what is right for you, just as I do what is right for me. But I can tell you that when people ask me if I do prints, and I say no, there is a huge sigh of relief - as well, you need to know that some galleries will not take you if you do prints. But again, you need to figure that one out for yourself.

A Compromise?

Perhaps you will do specific work intentionally created for mechanical prints, and these are your potstickers. If you want to step in to the print market, consider doing work that is specifically FOR prints - leave your "serious" work untouched.

If you do prints consider limiting the edition size to 100 or 250. There is an initial outlay for photographing the work, the printer costs etc and you have to consider if you will sell enough prints to make those funds back, and also be a successful revenue stream. Be cognizant that your potential client will be looking at the cost of your original, and also how much you are asking for the print of that work.

There is no real right or wrong answer - it depends on what your end goal is, what your vision is for your work. Stay true to yourself, and do what you need to do, and no one can say anything that really matters.

How Much Art Are You Donating?

Consider how much artwork you are giving away. Are you defeating the purpose of your selling work? If you are donating to every fund raiser, then why would someone want to buy your work from you, when they can get it for so much less at a fund raiser? This is such an important topic, a whole chapter is dedicated to the idea of donating art, and much discussion will be given there.

What Are Other Ways I Can Raise Money?

Workshops, grants, crowd source funding and sales are potential revenue generators. Workshops depend on your education or experience, or both. Places to give workshops include the local art centres, through art groups as a guest artist, or contact the local art supply stores. Create a mini 5 minute video online accessible through Youtube that is an advertisement for your actual workshop. Give a 5 minute art philosophy talk about why you create art. Have a small conversation with someone and post the video online. All of these demonstrate your verbal skills and will show someone what you would be like as an instructor. It's advertising.

What should you charging for workshops depends on the local economy, and what it will bear. Is it better to have ten students at $100 or 3 students at $200? There are many instructors out there, what makes you unique? Use that for your advertisements, but watch how much you charge. For advertising your classes, ask your cheerleaders (more later) for help, and get the word of mouth going.

Grants

"The global recession of the last few years has affected all sectors, including the arts. The Conference Board of Canada estimates that revenues for Canada's culture sector declined in 2009 by about $3.1 billion, or 4.3%. While recover is under way, governments at the federal, provincial and municipal levels are sending clear signals that several lean years lie ahead. This situation has a double effect on the Council. First, the Council's own revenues from government are unlikely to grow and may even be adjusted. Second, because the Council is a national arts funder, it is affected by decisions made by all levels of government. Cuts in arts funding elsewhere almost always lead to increased demand on the Council."[1]

At the back of the book is a list of arts funders by province and sometimes by city. In Canada, it is pretty lean for arts funders, and each one of those places will have a website dedicated to provide you information and forms for applying for grants. Simply said, it is very competitive, and I do not suggest relying on grants to complete your projects.

Many organizations have excellent grant writers, and if the magic words are spoken the grant is delivered. In my opinion there is a lot of trust given to arts organizations, and some misuse that trust. Because of such limited funds able to be given out to organizations and persons, I would like to see that all applicants would have to provide an actual current business audit.

---

1   Canada Council for the Arts, Strengthening Connections: Corporate Plan 2011–16 Summary page 3

Crowd Source Funding

A new way of funding projects is completely the result of the internet, and is called Crowd Source Funding. In the US and the UK, the host platform is Kickstarter and in Canada, it is called RocketHub.

Basically what happens, is you post up a project online, supported by video, auditory and written statements, you advertise it through your cheerleaders and their friends, called Backers, and you raise the funds you need. You keep 100% of your idea, and of your work.

There is no application fee, but there is a small commission on the back end, that is related to the amount of money that you were able to raise for your project. You control the funding goal, and the deadline. The idea is that people can become involved in your project, and if they believe in it and you, they will pledge money to make it happen.

Make sure you read everything in the costing sections. Ensure you know what the fees are, ensure you know what the limits are for percentages you have to pay, and ensure you understand that your project promises must be filled exactly as you stated. This is a contract binding between you and your Backer, and the trust implications are clear: for you as the artist, the Backer investing in you, and the host platform as well.

Backers are those who help spread the word. Backers do not receive a kick back, instead, you are the one who controls what gifts you give to thank your Backers. The thank you gifts are done in tiers, i.e. for $10 support, you will give a mention in the credits, for $20 you will give a print, or such. For $1000 you might do a commission for your backer. Larger pledges for you result in larger gifts for them. Be generous.

If you think about it, this is how many art projects were funded in the past. Large patrons, smaller patrons - they all believed in the artist, they were inspired or their imagination was captured by the possibilities generated by a particular project. Theoretically, everyone wants to back a winner, so get the word out by social media, word of mouth, a news release. Put a unique twist on what you are doing. Make it memorable, make it irresistible.

The amount of funds and the time needed for raising it depends on your project. It could be as little as $100 over a period of a month to $20,000 with a three to five month duration.

Consider that 1000 people supporting your project with $10 is much more likely to succeed than 3 people supporting with $500. The power of numbers are on your side.

Again, be generous. Treat your backers very well, you never know when your next project will need the help. If your Backer has a project, consider helping them out too.

Sales

Be smart about offering sales, and have a reason for them such as a sale in support of your art ventures. Time limited. Price limited.

Summary

Artists and other creative types are the ones who are the movers and shakers of the world. Don't be afraid to be seen moving and shaking... remember: market like no one is watching. Maybe it just takes your action to break down the barrier of what was never done in the past.

Sample Checklist

Here is the start of a sample checklist for putting together the marketing portion of your plan:

1. Paper Toolbox:
   - Biography
   - CV
   - Titles/Artist Statement
   - Inventory sheets

2. Where are you in the marketplace?

3. Are you marketing?

4. What marketing materials do I need?
   - Business Cards
   - Postcards

5. Are you doing potstickers?

6. Are you selling local?
   - If yes, where?
   - If yes, who are your audience/clients?

7. Are you selling on the internet?
   - If yes, where am I selling?
   - Who are my clients?
   - Do I have a blog or website?

8. What galleries am I interested in?
   - Where are they?

9. Where am I donating art and how much per year?

10. What are other ways I can raise funds?
    - Grants
    - Crowd Source Fundraising

Chapter 8 - Showing Your Work

Showing Your Work

Calls to Artists

There are normally two main goals when you submit work to a Call: exposure and sales (or for a CV listing perhaps). Why wouldn't you do the absolute best you can to satisfy and succeed in those two goals?

First thing: RESPECT the deadlines. That means you need to mark your own calendar, and be responsible for work drop off, and for work pick up.... on time! When I coordinate a show, I don't want you calling me every week and asking me when to drop off work, or when to pick up work, or even when the show is, when I have already provided you with that information or it's on the website. The excuse "I am an artist, I am above/I don't know how/can't/don't want to" is bullshit.

Make sure your artworks are labeled! For a few years, I had the opportunity to coordinate and curate the Evergreen Art Gallery at the Rotary Centre for the Arts here in Kelowna, of about 40 or 50 works - I would say at least 75% of the works were not marked on the back. Nothing. No title, no medium, no artist name, nothing. When the same artist submits five pieces, and none of them are marked, what do you think is the likelihood of the correct tag being put on the work? Or if an artist submits an unmarked diptych or a triptych, what is the likelihood that they will be arranged properly?

Obviously if the artist does not care to mark the piece, then should I care to make sure the right tag is on it, or it is in the right order?

Art and Respectability

I come from a very strict background on one hand, but a very free-flowing mindscape on another. My father was a stronghand, he had certain expectations that had to be met, he had certain values that he wouldn't tolerate being compromised. But one thing he always told me was to set my own rules. I didn't really understand what he meant because he wasn't a real good demonstration of this ideal, but I understand now, some years after his death, that was his heart and soul talking to me, and I am convinced that if he could do it over again, he would.

My years in the military taught me structure, taught me order, and what it was like to be confined. Now, I have been out of the military longer than in it (I retired in 97), and I am understanding more and more of what it means to make my own rules. I am understanding that the value of social pressure can be used for good, but it is also very detrimental. While it isn't quite "Lord of the Flies" here in the Okanagan, there is tremendous social pressure to conform, to only do certain things, to be friends with only certain people. I never bought in to that sort of thing, and here is where my realization lies. Social conformity suffocates creativity.

My mother had the type of attitude that as long as it didn't hurt anyone, anything goes, pretty much. All points of view are valid, it is just choosing which one you want to adopt and fits in with your life. Just because "I" make certain decisions, or ask certain questions, doesn't mean that YOUR decisions or actions are wrong.

I always have the most interesting conversations with my fellow artists because it always provokes further thought, and recently I had one about "quality" and "respectable" galleries and venues. Do you think that just because someone doesn't follow another's rules that their work lacks quality or respectability?

Standards - Rant

"Everybody is a genius. But if you judge a fish by its ability to climb a tree, it will live its whole life believing that it is stupid."
Albert Einstein

I wonder if it is better to be told that an artist needs to meet "standards" or if one should "make" those standards. Isn't it better to be wanted for who you are rather than be dictated to? Art is really a process that illuminates what is going on within, if we pay attention. For me, the process of working with clay for example, adding, subtracting, being malleable, and then solidifying over time, finally to firing, is a parable for social conformity. Now I am working with stone, carving out, revealing the subject within, chipping away the rigid boundaries - I'm seeing a parallel of a path to independence and maturity....

Regarding respectability, I don't think there is a correct answer, right for everyone. I only know the questions and comments I make to myself: By being told what standards you will adhere to, the walls of a box are created, and then you inhabit that box, but that is someone else's box. By defining what standards you adhere to, you become known for a certain thing. Is respectability all that it is cracked up to be? Does quality require respectability? Do you want to be respectable, or do you want to be alive and carefree and happy? Do you want people to want you for who you are or how you toe the line?

The Curator (if it is not you)

Sometimes the sad truth is that you may not like how a curator displays your work. You have the option to either see it as the curator sees it, or the message that the curator is trying to get across or understand how the curator had to work within the space confines, or you can take your work out. If you take your work out, you run the risk of looking like a high maintenance prima donna, or in my eyes, at the least, very unprofessional. But that is your choice. One piece of advice is to not be a pain and ask the curator to change their arrangement of your works.

When a curator is installing a show they have constraints such as space and what other works are submitted, at the very minimum. The best overall look for a show is the number one priority for the curator. Simply put, artist egos have no place in determining where an artwork goes. Larger works are usually placed first, or depending on the message that needs to be conveyed, the artworks that are placed first are usually the strongest in that message. Something I should say again, is that artist egos have no place in deciding where an artwork goes, most especially in a group show. Again, if you aren't the curator, then butt out.

When you submit work for a show, it is the curator's job to ensure it all works within the space and the artworks as a whole. The artist is responsible for their work arriving and departing, and the curator is responsible for the presentation. Make sure your art is labeled so the curator knows if pieces are to be displayed together. Always put a business card on the back of your artwork.

Present your best artwork in a professional manner at all times, and the curator will do their best too.

Showing Outside of Galleries

Think about where you can show your work outside of the galleries. These include places such as cafes or restaurants or other public spaces, offices or such. When you agree to show your work, be business minded. In supplying artwork for their walls, they receive a benefit, as do you, which is exposure and possible artwork sales.

The best way to not provide good service as an artist to your potential business partners is to never communicate, never provide updated contact information if you move or change phone numbers, and never follow-up on agreements to confirm that they are still in place or see if things have changed.

Example:
I was involved in a situation where, in December, an artist booked a space with a business for a May display. They never communicated with the business owner when they (the artist) moved, or even throughout the time leading up to their appointment to hang their artwork in May. I, on the other hand, went in sometime in March, to this same business, and asked if there were any spots available - I was told no, not until the fall, however, there is someone who was to go in May who they couldn't get in contact with.

Okay, I said to the business owner, I will follow up with you later on. I went back the end of March, and again once each week in April (a total of about four times from March to April) to find out what was happening. Finally, the last week of April I was given the go ahead because this other artist had apparently dropped off the ends of the earth. I contacted the currently displaying April artist for when they would be taking their work out. The two of us made arrangements, so that the business owner would not have bare walls for too long of a time.

Lo and behold, the lost artist came in on April 30th and was surprised to find that they lost their position.

Lessons learned:
1. Be interested in being able to show your work! Always follow up and/or confirm as time goes on.
2. Show interest in the business owner. Get to know them if you don't already patronize their business. Remember their clients will talk to the owner and ask them about your work. Give the owner something GREAT to say about you!
3. You are an artist and your communication is not restricted to the visual - communicate with the business owner, and the artist previous to you to make the transition as seamless as possible.
4. Always be professional.

Group Shows

Group shows are a terrific way to get your work up and on display. Tasks are normally shared equally and fairly. Artists count on each other. Group shows are also the most common way artists show their work. Your responsibility as an artist does not end with acceptance in to a show.

Do you know what your responsibilities are when in a group exhibition? The following are a list of questions to ask yourself if you are interested in doing a group show. Be honest with your answers.

1. Are you prepared to pull your own weight? I put a huge effort out to ensure the art shows I am involved in are successful. I have discovered (and endured much pain when I realized) that the reason a show is not successful, is not because of me.

2. Are you wishy washy and have a history of pulling out of commitments at the last second, or making some other excuse for bailing?

3. Are you prepared to show up at the show, 15 minutes early or are you always late?

4.   Are you prepared to contribute in equal terms of funding for advertising etc?

5. Are you prepared to be proactive and speak as nicely about my work as you are about your own?

6. Are you well versed in internet programs and opportunities, or are you interested to learn?

7. Are you able to think out of the box, or are you rigid?

8. Do you send out the info for the show, up to and including opening night and then let it go, waiting for (and/or expecting) others to advertise it further?

As I mentioned, in group shows, artists count on each other. The artworks are hanging side by side, and if one is getting more attention than yours, don't become defensive and not share the show because you are jealous. If it is one artist's turn for attention this time, eventually it will be yours. The worst enemy of artist to artist relationships is insecurity and its resulting jealousy. Your best friend can be your fellow artist.

The greater number of eyes means the greater potential for sales, for you and for everyone else. Fifty artists sharing the show info means a higher probability of success than one or two sharing the same info. If nothing else, do the math!

The opening night is only a small part of an art exhibition - the opening is where the works are introduced to the audience - but the remainder of a show is where artists remind the audience that their works are available. There should to be a gentle wooing relationship between artist and any potential buyer. Did you get a favourable response, and did someone like your work? Did you get an unfavourable response, and someone didn't?

Do the follow-up!

What is the Follow-up?

Maintaining a "relationship" with that someone in a general way just means that you remind people gently that the show is on, and that your work is in it. Re-tell your artist statement in a blog - expound on it a little more - talk about why you did the work, why you entered the show, what pushed you, give some insight, offer that little something that someone wouldn't know if they looked at the work. For someone who didn't like your work, address their thoughts, substantiate why you expressed as you did. People like to see people grow and expand. Are you shy? Well, good, because I am too!

Share!

Send out information once a week or so in various ways. Be excited! Those who are your true friends and supporters will know you are excited and be excited too! (The others, well, don't worry about them, you could put yourself in therapy if you did.) Once a week is not too much to let people know about a show that is on for a month.

Share!

Do you know how to use Facebook and/or Twitter? What a good time to learn, you only benefit yourself! These are tools that you can use to let people know your artwork exists. The world is not going to come knocking at your door, or as my dad used to say, "you owe the world, the world doesn't owe you!" Strong words, important words, pertinent words, especially in this day and age. If you are a professional artist, you have a responsibility to your own self to honour your works. I can sometimes tell how professional an artist is in the way that they advertise the shows they are in, whether it is their own work or someone else's....most especially someone else's.

When an artist is in a group show, I would expect this sort of support for your own artwork specifically, and the show in general. You entered, you were accepted, now go and encourage people to come and see it!

If Nothing Else, Do the Math

30 people in a month long exhibition, sent out once is 30 times in that month. 30 people in a month long exhibition sent out four times is 120 times in that month. Chances are that out of those 120 times, others will pick up and share the info, which has greatly increased the publicity of that exhibition and YOUR work. Remember that excitement is catchy. If you are enthused and excited about your work, and others will be too - it is unavoidable!

Self-Reliance

Artists are so easily convinced that their success is in the hands of another. I disagree with this. More artists need to take control of their careers - it makes me ask myself if they really do believe in themselves, or their work. Or are they just playing around?

How seriously are they taking THEMSELVES? Are they working to find their niche? Are they working at finding their voice? Are they working at finding themselves? Are they working at pushing past their boundaries?

Group shows exist, by their very nature, because of a group of artists. Wouldn't it make sense that these types of shows are more successful by the very involvement of these artists? I believe that those who do minimal effort, i.e. they submit and then sit back are likely going to be minimally successful.

Helping in a Group Show

Are you in a group show? Ask how you can help - your involvement does not stop with the submission of the artwork. Things you could do would be making labels, or registering the artwork, or helping for the few hours or so of being gallery host for the show, or helping to take it down. Compared to the many, many hours that the organizer puts in, your help would be invaluable, as well as indicating to the organizer you are interested in making the show a success too.

For those who sit back and let others do all the work, yet reap the benefits of the show, I add this attribute of their personality to their work, and yes, it makes me respect their work less. Brand is a verb not a noun.

Costs in a Group Show

Aside from the application fee, if the show is run by an artist or artist run gallery, then the expectation is that you will pay for the shipping to and from the show. If it is run by a commercial or public gallery then the expectation is that the artist will pay the shipping to the show, and the gallery will pay the way home. More on shipping will be under the Spending Money chapter.

All costs in a group show are expected to be split equally between the artists unless indicated otherwise, and in gallery shows, these costs are paid by the commission. (Here is a perfect illustration of why galleries are struggling today. If nothing or very little sells, the gallery has invested all the time and money and receives no income. It is no wonder why Vanity Galleries are popping up more and more.)

In an artist run show, costs may be covered by volunteering in lieu of money. That participation is invaluable to the person running the show, and makes it so much easier for the show to be successful without being a drain.

Chapter 9 - Pricing Your Artwork

Pricing Your Artwork

How do I price thee, let me count the ways.

How do you price your artwork fairly? This section might meander a bit, I am apologizing in advance, but you will see where I am going with it later.

Pricing is an uncomfortable subject. Art is very personal, and how can we be deserving of the price of it? We are in a creative field where "deserving" is a dirty word. Deserving is one word in which no one, as an artist (visual, performing or otherwise) in their right mind would ever admit out loud is part of their vocabulary when referring to themselves. People who work in other industries, for example, would have no problem saying "I deserve that raise" and likely get it, simply for standing up for themselves and making their needs known.

Providing these can be substantiated either with education or experience or ability, artists deserve the prices they put on their original works.

This concept is important enough that I need to repeat it: Providing these can be substantiated either with education or experience or ability, artists deserve the prices they put on their original works. Time to create an artwork is not a necessary factor to determine its price. It doesn't matter if it took me 5 minutes to create the work, 5 hours, 5 weeks or 5 months. The artwork is done when it says it is done, I really don't have much to say about it. A work that took 5 months could be seriously overworked, and a work that took 5 minutes could be overworked as well. There is a departing point where the artist is in control and then when the artwork takes over. Part of the skill of being an artist or even a creative being is knowing when that point is, when the point of the artwork being its own being has occurred.

I believe an originally executed artwork is an individual. Because of this individuality, the artwork deserves respect as its own being. Part of this respect includes giving it the recognition and honour in the outside world. Are you independently wealthy? Then anything you get for your work is a bonus, right?   79

A Bit of a Rant

As a professional artist, you make the artwork, you put a price on it. There are those people who will say "artworks from the heart have no price or are priceless". I say then that they do not need to make any money from their art to pay their bills and they do not need to rely on the sales of their work to survive and they are not a professional artist.

And, for those who say the artwork has no price, or is priceless, then by all means, pay me a million dollars for my work, because aren't you getting a great deal!

There are also artists who enter the field, and think they can claim top dollar for their work, because, well, those are the prices other artists are getting in the area. It doesn't work that way. Pricing for artwork is not the same as pricing for a toaster.

In our culture, in our society, art is not seen as hard work. Anyone can copy another's work - it takes eye and hand coordination, not brains and talent but, I challenge you to come up with a concept and an execution, pay for the supplies and the methods to market the work, not to mention the time to do all this, and tell me again how easy and inexpensive it is. It is no wonder why we price our works the way we do, and it is no wonder why we get upset when someone wants our artwork for free. I once had someone say that they didn't want to buy my work, they just wanted a workshop which was much cheaper, so they could do what I do. Seriously.

Let's talk about the laws of Supply and Demand before we get in to actual pricing.

The Laws of Supply and Demand

The four basic laws of supply and demand are:

1. If demand increases and supply remains unchanged, a shortage occurs, leading to a higher equilibrium price.
2. If demand decreases and supply remains unchanged, a surplus occurs, leading to a lower equilibrium price.
3. If demand remains unchanged and supply increases, a surplus occurs, leading to a lower equilibrium price.
4. If demand remains unchanged and supply decreases, a shortage occurs, leading to a higher equilibrium price.[1]

Depending on where you are in your career, you will find yourself in one of the Laws of Supply and Demand. Typically, an artist starting out, will be within Law 3. Law 4 could happen when you're dead. In my opinion, your goal is to get to Law 1. Start your prices low. Be realistic about where you are. Do your research. If you find your inventory growing, come back to these laws and see how you can make changes to improve your situation.

The Perfect Competitor

In art, the purchaser, in my opinion, is what microeconomics call the "perfect competitor" - this means that the purchaser is not reliant on the market price. The purchaser does not have to purchase the work, it is up to the artist to make the work desirable, and to state why the work is the price it is. You are your brand.

The following are the factors of supply and demand. These are what determines a successful sale.

---

[1]   Besanko & Braeutigam (2005) p.33.

Demand

The determinants of demand are the buyer's variables to purchase:

1. Income
2. Tastes and preferences
3. Prices of artworks
4. Subjects and prices of competitor artworks
5. Number of potential buyers

Supply

The determinants of supply are:

1. Production costs: how much a good costs to be produced i.e. the cost of labor, capital, energy and materials. How much art can you make, how much does it cost, how much time?
2. Number of artist competitors.

Never Underestimate Your Buyer's Intelligence

Do not start your prices too high. If you start your prices high, with no sales, you will have too much inventory. If you start your prices low, your work may sell faster, which will allow your work to get out in the general population and make your name.

If you think that you will establish a following with high prices, which say your art is exclusive only to the wealthy, that is a huge gamble and one that should be made carefully. Some people (including artists) think that low prices mean low quality. This is the furthest from the truth.

Never underestimate the intelligence of your potential buyer and try to blow smoke up their ass. Yours are not the only artworks out there, and the world is full of artists just as special as you. Be realistic about your prices. Art is no different than the corporate world where working from the bottom up is the norm. Not many people come in at the top floor.

82

Where you sell will also factor in to your prices. If you sell local only, you are limited to what is available in your area. If you sell worldwide, ie on the internet, that is another set of buyers open to you, but be consistent with your prices whether local or not.

Should I Put My Prices for my Artwork Online?

Some say yes, some say no. I think much depends on what your philosophy is, or if you are bound by any commercial gallery agreements.

I do, simply because I try to make things as easy as possible for people to purchase. I know that if someone has bought my work in the past, they are familiar with the quality, and more often than not, they will buy it pretty quickly after they decide they like or want it. Many of my clients are from word of mouth, and they've seen my work at their friends' place.

Some galleries do not want prices online because they prefer the client contact them directly for information. I made the mistake fairly early on where I gave internet exclusivity for my charcoal drawings. That meant that my drawings were only available through one channel on the internet. That was a big mistake, and one I will not repeat. My income was cut down to almost nothing, and it was at that point that I realized how much power I had in my hands with the self marketing.

Let's get to pricing.

The Actual Methods of Pricing

There are lots of different ways to price: by size, by time, by subject matter, but never by venue. Prices must be the same across the board. Choose one and stick with it for an entire body of work. If you do prints then you might want to consider how to price your prints. Prints should be substantially less than the originals, regardless if hand embellished or not. I would suggest you take three works, of different sizes (small, medium and large) and work out the prices according to the methods below. Then go back to your research of what other artists are selling at, and find out where your prices fit that way, or find a method of pricing that will work for you.

There are two streams of thought about pricing. The first is that pricing low will sell more works, but volume sold will compensate for the lower prices. The second is that pricing low will allow more of your artwork to go to the "less sophisticated" buyers, and repel the clients who require spending a ton of money on an artwork. I am not sure I support the last. "Bargain basement" low pricing may discourage a few buyers, but I think there are those who are more interested in finding the "next big thing", and will be able to say, I saw them first. That's a fairly hefty claim to make in today's art world. More work sold is better for you. So decide on your strategy. You have to be comfortable with it.

Pricing by Time

Pricing by time has to do with how much time you've put into the project and also what you intend on paying yourself per hour plus materials. Consider this to be the most commercial way to price your artworks. It is like a traditional job, you need to figure out how much you're worth, you are your own employer.

Two good resources are Art Marketing 101 by Constance Smith and The Business Side of Creativity, by Cameron S Foote. I highly recommend their purchase.

Down to the Details

You will need to figure out how many pieces you need to complete in a month. You will need to figure out how many you must sell on average to make your income goal. Are you selling original works at your price points? Are these sales often and consistent? How do you feel about prints? Usually they are sold for much less and are more affordable, but you will need to decide what your philosophical attitude is towards the print market. You may also have to get a day job, whether full or part time, to pay the bills until your career is established.

Calculations

1. Work backwards from a yearly standpoint. How much are you spending per year for your creative practice? Divide that by twelve, per monthly. This gives you your monthly business expenses.

2. Be realistic about how much you want to make per hour.

3. How many hours does it take to create an artwork? If you work in many different media, take an average of all three, or if dramatically different, then consider them separately.

4. Multiply your wage per hour by the hours to create an artwork. How many artworks do you need to do in a month, to make sure your expenses are covered?

5. Multiply the result in #4 above by 2. This will give you your profit. Yes, you are allowed to make a profit, don't feel bad about it.

6. Framing is always extra. Framing is usually the cost of the framing doubled, and added to the artwork. Some galleries triple this. Remember if you are paying commission on the framed work to the gallery, to factor this amount in to the final price.

7. Remember to consider commission from galleries, credit cards or other payment processors. Deduct that amount from your final price arrived at in #6, that's what you will receive. Are you happy with this amount?

Pricing by Size

The following guidelines are for unframed works. Pricing by size is a bit little bit more complex. Pricing by size could be either linear inches or square inches. Linear inches means length plus width multiplied by a factor of X, Y or Z. Square inches is length multiplied by width multiplied by a factor of X, Y or Z.

Prices need to be consistent across sizes. Choose a system for the unframed work i.e. Linear or Square. From your research for example, you will know what your 16"x20" should be. Decide what X will be to give you the price for that 16"x20", then you can decide what Y and Z will be. The nice thing about pricing by size is that you can increase your prices as you become more well known simply by increasing the factors, and the price increases are then very logical and can be planned.

Here are a few examples:

Where the Factors of X Y and Z Are the Same:

Linear Inches:

	Size	Factor	Resulting Price
Small	8" + 10" x Y	Y = 10	$180
Medium	16" + 20" x X	X = 10	$320
Large	30" + 40" x Z	Z = 10	$700

Square Inches:

	Size	Factor	Resulting Price
Small	8" x 10" x Y	Y = 1	$80
Medium	16" x 20" x X	X = 1	$320
Large	30" x 40" x Z	Z = 1	$1200

Where the Factors of X Y and Z Are Different:

Linear Inches:

	Size	Factor	Resulting Price
Small	8" + 10" x Y	Y = 8	$144
Medium	16" + 20" x X	X = 10	$320
Large	30" + 40" x Z	Z = 12	$840

Square Inches:

	Size	Factor	Resulting Price
Small	8" x 10" x Y	Y = 1.5	$120
Medium	16" x 20" x X	X = 1	$320
Large	30" x 40" x Z	Z = .5	$600

Why do the factors for X, Y and Z go up in Linear but in Square go down? It has to do with the resulting price itself. These are examples only, and your factors may be different depending on what your market research tells you.

In which range of prices does your work fit? You may also see that as your work raises in value, the factors of X, Y and Z are easily changed to accommodate the increase. And remember that commission? If you are in a gallery, and your gallery takes 50%, then you would receive half of the overall price.

This is why it is so important to do your research, find out where you are in terms of what prices you can get for your artwork. It may mean you do not sell in a certain field i.e. locally, or a gallery. If you are in a gallery, rely on their market information to tell you what your work will likely sell at. Ultimately, however, it is your decision.

Raising Your Prices

Over a period of time, it is generally expected, but not required, that your prices raise as demand increases for your work. Raising prices is based on the economic factors of supply and demand which were discussed earlier.

Is there demand for your work? Are you meeting the demand with the supply? Do you have a surplus or a deficit?

Using the formulae given, you have the ability to raise your prices dispassionately and objectively by changing the factors of X, Y and Z. It is said that you can always raise your prices, but it is harder to bring them back down. Regardless if you agree with this or not, raise your prices carefully and with much thought. This is something that should be built in to your map.

Framing

Framing can be a testy subject. It's expensive.

To frame or not to frame? That is the question. What type of frame? What colour, what style? Frames can enhance the work, there is no question of that. Work can be sold without frames. The frame you choose may not be the frame the buyer likes, and they will change it anyway if they don't like it, and you will have spent that money for nothing. The standard for frames is to work out the price of the art, then double the cost of the frame, and add it to the work.

So if the work price is $100, and the frame cost is $10, double the frame cost, and add it to the work, so the complete framed work is now $120.

Take the time to find a wholesale framer. You can save a lot of money. As well, regardless if professional or not, at any framer, ask them if they have any standard size ready-made frames available. These are made of left over ends, and are all new, all very good quality. When you price your artwork with that frame, include how much that frame would have cost at regular price.

Framing does allow a bit of wiggle room on prices. If you have a client who comes in and wants your "best deal" then you can offer them a reduction within the space of the framing.

Commissions

Commissions factor in to pricing in a big way. Commissions are something the galleries do charge and can range anywhere from 10% to 50 or even 60% depending on the gallery. If you're in a large market such as New York or even Vancouver, perhaps a 50 or 60% commission is valid but if you're in a smaller market like where I am, I feel that those commission prices are too high. You must factor in the commission prices of artworks though if you sell in a gallery, and this definitely affects the bottom line of what you will receive for your artwork. If you take the 30x40 unframed work above, with the constant linear inch factor of 10, and a retail price of $700, that means you would receive $350 for that artwork.

If you put your work in a gallery, and it is framed, then triple the cost of the framing and add it to the artwork cost. The reason for this is that you are paying the gallery commission on the frame too.

Summary

There is no such thing as failure, only results.
Anthony Robbins

You are more powerful than you think. Commissions from galleries can equate to commissions paid from paypal, website costs etc. Remember much of selling artwork is hit and miss. If you don't get your work out there, you won't be seen. 98% of your success is up to YOU! If you try something and it doesn't work, then try something else. Be consistent with your pricing: decide, act, evaluate.

Chapter 10 - Cheerleaders

Cheerleaders

Cheerleaders are found in real life and also on the internet. These are any people who encourage you onwards, whether by buying your work, or encouraging you to improve through guidance or competition. Value everyone you come in contact with, you never know who is going to be the old fairytale woman (or man) on the road who needs a meal.

Appreciate those who buy your work. Keep in contact with them. With so many artists in the world, and so many options to choose from, clients look for works that make them think or feel good. When they look at your work, enable them to feel good about it and you. Most people like to help a winner, so be a winner!

Cheerleaders can also be considered Stakeholders. Stakeholders are the ones who are interested in seeing a project or person in whom they believe, succeed. Stakeholders can be yourself, friends, family, your community, your buyers, organizations you belong to, the media and maybe even your competition. Never be afraid of competition, it can help you grow and expand.

You Need to be Your Own Cheerleader First

I have had many people, local and otherwise, tell me what a great marketer I am. It took me a while to realize that what I think they were really saying was how egotistical I was. Marketing, though, has nothing to do with ego, and everything to do with creating successful environment for your work.

Regardless of what job you are in, whether as an artist or a financier, if you don't believe in your abilities first, and don't stand up for yourself first, no one else is going to do it for you. You have to make yourself relevant. Market like no one is watching. Cheerleaders want to cheer, so give them something to cheer about. You are the brand. You are a verb, not a noun.

Make Yourself Relevant

Using myself as an example, I am interested in my community. I am interested in making a difference if I can. I have a big mouth, and if something does not seem right, I say so. If I see a fellow artist or an artist group being taken advantage of, I say so. I don't say things to be controversial: there is no goal of trying to be in front of the media. I say because I care, because I get frustrated with the ignorance of how artists (or others) are treated - whether through their own devices or having it inflicted upon them, making them the "victim".

Everyone knows the story of Van Gogh and how he was the "victim" of his society. Artists these days have no need of being victims of anything except of themselves. And that is truly a choice. Next time you think "they" are against you, think who exactly are "they"? It just might be yourself in disguise.

Buyers

The best rule I know is that if a person sees an artwork and they can not forget it, then that artwork is destined to become theirs. If they talk to you about it at a later date, offer a layaway plan if they can not afford it outright. Make it obtainable. Sometimes offering your buyer a percentage off if they buy x number of dollars worth is a good idea.

Designers will always buy artwork. Joe Public will buy artwork. I offer designers the wholesale price (the retail price minus 30%) because I consider that similar to a gallery commission. Designers believe in your work enough to buy it outright. I value them highly.

Organizations

An art organization can also be considered a cheerleader. These are usually established with the artist's best interests at heart in response to a need or a reaction to events. In Canada, the organization CARFAC - Canadian Artists' Representation/Le Front des artistes canadiens http://www.carfac.ca/ is the best one I have seen so far. Research their beginnings, it is quite interesting. Non Profit art galleries and art associations are also excellent resources. Arts Councils, art organizations run by artists - look to see what your community has to offer. And if there is none for the need you have identified, start one yourself!

Competition

With the internet, and the ability of Joe Public being able to search for artworks instantly across the globe, competition for the art buyer has been taken to a new level. With so many artists being internet savvy and using metatags efficiently, it is easy to pull up artworks in Google Images with the tags "original art, acrylic painting, female nude, expressionism".

We all need to work together, we all need to stand on each other's shoulders. A helping hand up the ladder does not mean someone will pass you, it means that you are secure enough to share space. So share. Competition is healthy for all of us, and keeps us on our toes. It sharpens us, it softens us. Don't be afraid of it.

Sharing

Friends are as companions on a journey, who ought to aid each other to persevere in the road to a happier life.
Pythagoras

The internet is about sharing, and in an ideal world this would happen. I can count on one hand the other artists doing it - and I can count on two fingers the number of traditional businesses who do it for others, especially their competition. Not many others are doing it.... and I came to wonder .... why?

Why Can't This Be a Mutual Admiration Society?

Are people so afraid to point "their" public in another's direction? Are people so worried that their own income will be sacrificed if someone else is promoted? I would like to see the local community support the local community. If you are on Facebook, what would it cost you to hit the SHARE button on your friend's events and happenings and press enter? Would it REALLY hurt you to hit the RT button on Twitter?

Consider that if you help others, even those who are not your close friends, you help yourself.

Business Cards

People who allow you to leave your business card on their premise are also cheerleaders.   Consider the following places to leave your cards:

Libraries
Doctor's & Dentists offices
Schools
Gyms
Restaurants
Community centers
Coffee shops
Grocery stores
City hall
Parks
Framing shops
Hair salons and/or spas
Child care centers
Art galleries
Children's gyms/activity centers
Auto repair shops
Real estate offices
Churches
Bookstores
Community colleges
Malls

Media

This last group of cheerleaders but certainly one of the most important is that of the media. They are always interested in what you are doing in the community, most especially as volunteers. They care about their community as much as you do, and I believe, perhaps naively some will say, that they wish to influence it for the positive as well. This not to say that some don't have political aspirations, but I prefer to think of the media as those who wish to make their community better.

The media may help you with your projects, they may do an interview or mention what you are doing in an article on art. There are quite a few reporters and editors who are very strong arts advocates in my community, and I bet it will be easy to find them in yours too. You just have to look and ask them if they are interested in what you are doing. Explain how it is relative to the community and for public interest.

The City You Live In

Where I live, the City has invested a great deal of time and interest in the cultural health of our community. Thanks to the dedication of a number of individuals and over many years, the City has committed to a Cultural Plan that will see our creative community thrive.[1]

The City of Kelowna has now dedicated funds to aid arts organizations (not individuals) and the attitude is one of how can we help you? I think that is terrific, and I am glad to think there are also some rules/guidelines/audits in place that will prevent the City from being hosed by those who "say" they are advocates when in fact they are just looking out for their own pockets. Art and culture are big business.

---

1   Kelowna Cultural Plan: 2012-2017, Thriving, Engaging, Inspiring

Chapter 11 - Charity and Donations

Charity and Donations

Introduction

I have had quite a few experiences with donating art. I will list a few of them here, as well as comments I have had with art patrons, their views on art auctions, and how things can change for the better.

How Did This All Start?

The economy for the past twenty years has been such that the gaps between the haves and the havenots have gotten wider. The creatives, whether right-brain creatives or left-brain, are the ones who are most likely to donate from the heart.

We care about our society, we are more likely to empathize with our fellow human or animal, and we want to help. Many of us don't have a great deal of money, and how else to contribute to a hearty cause than to give work from our own.

People attend the fundraisers because they also care (or the cynic might say they just wish to be seen) and here we have the birth of silent auctions. Where it used to be that patrons of the fundraisers tried to outbid each other and were generous with their funds in the spirit of the fundraiser, the current attitude has changed to one of conservative stinginess. I mean, why even bother going then?

Stepping Up to the Plate

At Night of the Arts, a local fund raiser, always for a worthy cause, and put on entirely by artists, coordinated by local personality Charlie Hodge, was quoted in the newspaper as saying "it is the artist every time that steps up to the plate". Yes it IS the artist who steps up to the plate, because we know what it is like to have nothing, and hope, (though some may deny this), that maybe, just maybe, through the charity's nebulous promise of exposure, someone will search us out and actually purchase an artwork from us because they like our work.

It hardly ever happens.

Why?

I believe a number of factors are at play here:

- social mindset that local art is somehow inferior
- social mindset of art at silent auctions "where's the deal"
- social mindset that they'll just get it at another time in another silent auction

Note I said social mindset, and a social mindset is something that can be altered, but it takes the local society to accomplish this. We can make it happen, it just requires the determination and steadfastness.

Local Art is Inferior? - Rant

Local artists are the grass roots of the city, the people who support the community even when they really can't afford to, and I wouldn't be surprised to find many of them at the Food Bank. Yet we give and give and give. What comes back? Some good karma, eventually, I guess. Maybe this lifetime or the next, but how well does that pay this month's bills? Try taking that to the bank.

It seems art is only valued if you pay for it. The same people who attend $250 a ticket dinners have no problem going in to the commercial galleries and spending thousands of dollars there, yet at the fundraiser they ask "Where's the deal?" when an artist, out of the goodness of their heart, has donated a work.[1]

If my work is good enough for your silent auction, isn't it good enough for you to purchase? I am so tired of being told, "I'm going to wait til the next silent auction to pick up a piece of yours". I've also been told, "oh yes, I am going to buy a piece after you donate to my fund raiser." That worked on me a total of ONE time.

---

1   Actual conversation with Tracie Ward, ED of RCA when discussing the Rotary Centre for the Arts Evergreen Fundraiser, $250 a plate dinner.

Donating Artwork

If you do want to donate, consider the following questions:

1. Do you support the cause that they are promoting?
2. Do you want to feel involved?
3. Do you **need** to contribute?

The act of donating is a heart AND a mind decision.

Typically the non profits that give the receipts for income tax are registered with government and I highly recommend you look them up on the Canada Revenue Agency website and make sure that their charity in good standing and see exactly what it is that they spend their money on. You can look at the past reports under their name and see exactly where their dollars are going.

Be aware of the misconception that if the artwork is donated for their specific event that you have just given the artwork to them forever and ever. Some non profit art galleries respectfully ask if the artwork does not sell during this particular event can they keep it for another event. You do have the choice of saying yes or no. You need to make sure you do your due diligence to make sure that there is no misunderstanding.

I've sat on a number of fund raising committees where the discussion goes around who could we get to donate, and with art being the number one easy donation with the least amount of work. That's why there is so much artwork at a silent auction.

Exposure

Never ever believe the verbal hype given that you will get "exposure". It's a fallacy, a lie, a misnomer, a misdirection. Don't believe it. It's bull shit. Can I say it any clearer?

If on the other hand, you have a written agreement regarding the publicity, i.e. your name included in press releases, posters, documentation, and such, then yes, that is exposure.

104

This is not about ego. It's about business.

Implications on Income Tax

Charities registered with the Canada Revenue Agency are required to follow specific rules when it comes to art donations. If the art donation is over a certain value, there are standards that must be met, such as gallery appraisals or other appraisals. These appraisals are generally paid for by the artist, and the appraisals can come from the gallery the artist is in, or a non profit art gallery famliar with the artist's work.

One thing that I myself do is I make sure that the nonprofit will be able to give me at least at the very least a tax receipt that I can use on my income tax. Tax receipts can only be given from non profits who are registered with the CRA. More information on charitable tax receipt implications can be found on the government websites.[2]

Speaking of income tax, did you know that professional artists are among the lowest income levels for all of Canada? According to Hill Strategies, the average income for artists in Kelowna was just over 17K in 2006. Yet, we are the ones who are asked over and over again for art donations to support the many worthy non profit societies in our town. I highly doubt that the Kelowna artist experience is peculiar to Kelowna.[3]

---

2   CRA (Canada) http://www.cra-arc.gc.ca/chrts-gvng/dnrs/menu-eng.html,
IRS (US) http://www.irs.gov/publications/p526/ar02.html
3   http://hillstrategies.com/sites/default/files/Artists_large_cities2006.pdf

Why Donate?

Even before 2004, I have been vocal about my dislike of silent auctions and art. I have been vocal to artists encouraging them to be smarter about who they donate to, and to make their donation relevant. The following are some harsh opinions about donating art, but I will try to say them as diplomatically as I can.

The attitude from many of the charitable organizations is that we artists should feel blessed that we are donating out of the goodness of our heart, and any reference to business or cash or income is distasteful. From my point of view, this attitude shows the lack of education and awareness of the committee members but that they recognize art is a valuable commodity…. as long as it is free to them.

The first question that comes to my mind is why are they asking for art? Is the non profit a cultural entity? For example, is it a non profit art gallery asking for an artwork, and does that art gallery support YOU **specifically** as an artist? If so, then I feel it would be an excellent way to support them too, it shows that you believe in each other.

Artists are often asked by friends who are supporting a charity to give an artwork for that friend's charity. There is a little bit of pressure to conform there, I think. There is an old adage about friends and money, and it is a true one, lasting the ages.

It is better to go out and decide on your own what charity to help out, talk to that charity one on one, and make an agreement with them that you will support them, and that they support you. Perhaps choose two or three to work with over the year, and develop a relationship with them. Let them know your needs too as you try to help them. Make it personal. A one sided relationship is not fulfilling. It has to be a win win situation.

This is one of the important times in your life where you can't cave in to perceived social pressure. Hold on long enough and the social pressure you are feeling right now will be turned back to the fund raisers. The perceived social pressure will require them to treat you fairly.

And why shouldn't it? Art is hard work.

It is my contention that the social mind set regarding art at fund raisers, and I am told by artist friends around the globe, that the Okanagan is not special in all this, is one of "Where's the deal?" We need to change the social mind set of donating to charities. Charities are big business, don't fool yourself otherwise. Consider the fact that if they are able to give a tax receipt, they are a business whether they admit it to you, or not. As a professional artist, you need to be a business too.

Some non profits try to make you feel bad if you stand up for yourself, or your art, and if you do not go along with their request, well you aren't really that altruistic, it's about your ego and you're just out for the money, aren't you?

Case Study

Recently I received a Call to Artists from a local arts group. Although this group claims that they are an advocate for artists, when they pass on Calls to Artists that basically says, "here artist give your artwork away for free", I don't consider that to be an advocate. I understand these processes are changing with more discernment being given to Calls. I hope so.

This Call to Artists came from a non profit entity relating to health care which brings in a ton of funds to help the local health care industry. The non profit itself has the Board of Directors and on the Board of Directors are professional people such as doctors, lawyers etc. It has a wonderful set of web pages full of the donations from all people who believe in them. I believe in their mission too, I just don't agree with what they are doing to the local artists. This Call to Artists has been done for the past ten or so years and goes something like this:

...every year we have a juried competition to select an artwork from an artist to put in our Pediatric area. It must be framed, matted and will be on display for x amount of time. The successful artwork is going to have prints made of it, and will be given to the donors who donate that year to our non profit...

The problem I have with this Call to Artists is that they are asking for a free artwork (regardless of the age of the artist), they are asking the artist to pay for matting and framing (upwards of a few hundred dollars), and even after this financial outlay, the artist may not even be the one chosen for the "exposure" of prints made for their work. In addition, prints of the artwork will be given as a gift to the "real" donors, but no reimbursement for reproduction rights to the artist.

What is the gift to the successful artist? Can you imagine if the successful artist is a young person? What is the message being given to this young person?

If you are interested in reading about this particular Call to Artists, please go to my website and click on the Press Section, look for the article titled **Art for Free**. It will give you quotes from the non profit entity who's Executive Director said he did not receive my emails regarding this Call. I wrote him the second time offered to help change their Call to be more artist/business friendly, and included his President and Vice President as a cc. Amazingly enough, he received that email just fine! Lesson learned: when contacting an ED of an organization, cc their President and Vice.

The Follow Up

I had been waiting to hear from the media about who won the Call to Artists from the non profit. There was nothing in the media that I could see. I was having lunch with my artist friend, Rebekah Wilkinson, who filled me in with the details, and I trust that they are very accurate details, because she was the one who won the competition. There are a few other factors I am not going to go into, just the major ones, and yes, I am being very critical of the process in place. There is no excuse in this city, supposedly so culturally aware, for artists to be treated so poorly.

Framing: This artist spent just about $250 to have the work matted and framed, and the non profit did not like the matting and framing, and asked that it be redone. How would you feel about that request?

Publicity/Exposure: The announcement of the winner of this Call to Artists was held at a small coffee shop downtown next to the radio station that was the sponsor. Six pieces were submitted and on display. She tells me there was nothing published that she could find in any newspaper, but apparently her work was mentioned in the national e-newsletter of the sponsor, that went out to all the radio station subscribers, with an image of her work, but not her name. No links to her website, no other publicity that she could find. On the non profit's website, there is a tiny hidden obscure page with a small image of her artwork and her name is in little letters. If that is exposure, then I've been doing it wrong all these years.

Tax Receipt: A tax receipt was promised and it is up to the artist to provide the non profit with a gallery appraisal. The target audience for this Call to Artists are "new emerging local artists"[4]. These are artists who are not likely to be with a gallery. The artist was told by the local public art gallery curator that if the artist is not with a gallery, an "official" gallery appraisal could cost $500 with a lawyer. This artist was also told she would need sales receipts from previous art sales, a damage report that a gallery owner has physically seen the piece and that it is in good condition, all on company letter head. Considering that the non profit had taken possession of the work, and it was not offered to her to obtain this gallery appraisal, she is at a loss as to how she would get the tax receipt promised. As a new emerging artist, would you spend $500 to get a gallery appraisal?

Instead

Instead, why can they not have artists submit artworks, unframed, unmatted, to be considered for the process, choose an artwork, and then PAY the artist (regardless of their age) a stipend which would cover the price of the artwork and the privilege for the non profit to make prints of the selected work? Reproduction rights are a serious amount of cash for an artist. Having been on a non profit board with a fraction of the budget that this health care non profit has, there is definitely an ability to work in $1000 in to the budget to ensure the artist is given a fair shake. We've done it at the Okanagan Military Museum and I know others have as well. It is do-able and fair.

---

4   National Corporate Newsletter of Astral Radio

By paying the artist, the statement of "you respect and value us enough to donate, and we are going to value and respect your work in return".

Can you imagine if the successful artist is a young person? What is the message being given to this young person?

The Meat and Potatoes of Art Auctions by Charities: Reserves, Silent Auctions, Live Auctions, Mystery Bids

Reserves

All art auctions should have reserves. The reserves should be set by the artist. The charity needs to honour those reserves. If the reserve is not met, the artwork is not sold and is returned to the artist unless otherwise agreed upon in writing by the charity and the artist.

Reserves should be the lowest price you, as the artist, are comfortable with for letting that artwork go. It should be up to the artist to determine where the artwork should start at, not the charity.

Case Study

I no longer support art galleries who do not stand up for the artist nor respects art work. In 2012, I was involved with a local non profit art gallery who did not honour my reserve, and sold the artwork for less than my stipulated price. This is the note I sent to the gallery after I was asked for a donation in 2013:

I donated for the last two years to the xxx Art Gallery. That first year, I saw how low the artwork was being purchased. While mine went for a reasonable price, I saw how horrible and disrespectful the bids were for other artists' work, knowing that it could be me in that position. I did not like that feeling and I did not accept that a public art gallery, who is supposed to by an advocate for arts and artists, would accept that either.

The next year, which was 2012, I put on my form that a reserve was required to be met in order for the work to be sold. The reason I did that is because that particular work was at Gallery Odin in a past show, as well as requiring that people who attend auctions not think that the art there is at a garage sale. I was astonished that the reserve requirement was ignored. I wrote the xxx Art Gallery, and asked why, with no response, as well as asking to see the Executive Director, who was not available for an artist who supported the gallery. These kinds of actions are not something I can accept. I am no longer donating to the xxx Art Gallery.

I got a response fairly quickly from the Executive Director and we had a lengthy discussion. I understand that their policy has now changed, and was told they are now honouring the reserves as set by the artist.

Silent Auctions

Silent Auctions do have pros and cons.

What I like about Silent Auctions is that people get to dream about owning an artwork by a specific artist - whether it's me or someone else, it doesn't matter; they get to dream and dreams are very important.

What I don't like about Silent Auctions is that your artwork could be placed next to a toaster, and the toaster might go for more than your work. Minimum bids are fine for getting people going, but too often nowadays, it is the artwork that gets sold out for the minuscule amount of money that would come in to the non profit. **Sold out**. Yep, I said it. For all that we believe in "culture", art is **sold out**.

I would like Silent Auctions if those attending got into the spirit of the event, and weren't cheap. Some view silent auctions like a garage sale.

Case Study

For example, in Penticton a few years ago, there was a lovely graphite drawing by Nick Bantock (of Gryphon and Sabine fame) up for bid at a non profit art gallery. The starting bid was fairly low, I think it was $30 or $50, something crazy like that. The first bidder started out with a substantial bid and then scratched it out, and entered the starting bid instead. As well, near the end of the auction, they stood in front of the artwork to "block" any further bids. I dashed a last minute bid in, definitely on the line of the final bidding call, but substantially higher than theirs, and I won the drawing. If they hadn't cheaped out, and kept to their original more generous bid, I would never have been able to win the artwork. Note to patrons: it is not a garage sale, it is a fund raiser, so bid high and often.

The Future of Art in Silent Auctions

It is always the same people that I see on the community boards doing the non profit fund raising and who are the ones buying or not buying the works. After 10 years of how many silent auctions, how many people have room on their wall for all these artworks? They don't. That's why artworks are not selling in Silent Auctions anymore.

I believe silent auctions are now passé. Silent Auctions are no longer the ideal for raising money and non profits. In our own area, the Okanagan, artists give away so much work (it seems to me) that I do not wonder about the lack of investment value for the local population.

There are two public art galleries in the Okanagan who offer the artist a percentage of the amount raised. The artist can choose a value between 30 to 70 percent. That's a good start, but in my opinion, not good enough. There are too many hoops for the artist to jump through.

If people can no longer get your work for free, you will have contributed to the education and awareness of collectors understanding that art costs to make - in skill, time and money and each piece is the culmination of your life experience. Could you have done that same piece five years ago? Art is hard work. If you value your work, others will too.

112

Mystery Bids

There's another suggestion that has come up recently regarding Mystery Bids as a way of auctioning artwork. The artwork is still on for auction however as a Mystery Bid no one can see another's bid. If the value of your work is retail $500 and the reserve is $250, which in my opinion would be the minimum fair reserve, then the highest amount bid over the reserve is what the work is sold for. It really is a lot of fun because no one can see each other's bids, unlike the Silent Auction sheet which is open for all to see. It is for the true art lover and supporter who realizes well, I really like that and I really want to support the artist and I want to support the nonprofit, and I'm here for a fund raiser, gosh darn it!

Creative Solutions

One local group is taking this mentality and putting an artistic spin on it, in hopes to raise awareness, generate funds for local feline friends and create support for their cause. The AlleyCATS Alliance, a cat support group opened a call for artists to submit electronic images of some of their cat-based artwork, which was then voted on online. The top 52 choices were put into the 2013 AlleyCATS calendar. The only thing the artist donated was a printable jpg. They kept the artwork for sale, it cost them nothing, got their artwork in front of people who are interested in their subject matter and raised funds for the animal group. Win / win.

My Ideal Solution

What I would like to see for non profits who ask for artwork is that a patron who would normally support the arts, or a board member buy the artwork and then donate it to their charity. The artist gets the sale, the charity gets the work to sell off, and the patron or board member gets the tax receipt from the charity for their income tax.

Everybody wins.

Patrons

I would love to see the patrons and supporters of a non profit entity who takes artwork as a form of a fund raising initiative, and ask that non profit entity if they have paid the artist, how much, and to openly criticize the non profit if they have not. Change can be done.

Community Work

Never underestimate the power of an artist in the community. Help your community out. Make smart decisions about this though, and don't buy in to the "exposure" argument. You are a business person, and always stand up for yourself, because no one else will. For a city that prides itself for being so culturally aware, I think it's rather sad that artwork is undervalued at non profit events and fund raisers.

Summary

What will the next generation say about the non profits who approach artists of all types, and with a tug on the heart strings, request artists to donate their art for their cause, without recompense? What will the next generation say about the artists who give in for the illusion of "helping", or "exposure" and the dream of "promotion"?

I would like to see a strong statement made by the patrons who support the non profits, and who also support the Arts, whether it is music, art or drama, by standing up and saying to these non profits "you will see no more of my funds until you pay the artists and give them the respect they deserve"....

Is that a dream? Maybe. But I am a dreamer, and I believe it can be so.

Chapter 12 - Art and the Internet

Art and the Internet

The Economy

The economy has been really tough since 2008 on those of us who pay our bills from the results of artwork sales. I mean, really tough. Talk about going in to a black hole of nothingness. So what do you do? Do you complain and sit back and say, it's the economy...? If big works aren't selling, make small ones. If paints cost a lot of money, learn to use another medium that doesn't cost a lot. Explore, be inventive, go beyond the apparent barriers, and you will surprise yourself. Make noise - eventually it will turn into song.

Does Artwork Really Sell Online?

Yes, it does. There is no other way to say it. I remember back in 2004 when I was looking for a way to get my work out of the Okanagan, and I started to sell on eBay. Sure eBay wasn't the regular route, but it has never been my path to go the regular route. I was doing very well - my first piece was $900 30x40 oil painting to a fabulous woman in Ontario, and it only increased from there.

Later in 2004 or early 2005, I remember going to a marketing seminar "Are you Export Ready", put on by the local artist run gallery. I was told at that time I was not export ready, even though I had already sold more than a couple thousand dollars worth in the few months that I was online. I attended the seminar to learn about exports and regulation, and learned enough to find the rest of the way myself. Anyway, I digress. There was a discussion about where to put artworks for sale, and someone at the back said "you can always sell on eBay!" Everyone laughed as if it was a big joke. I was very hurt by that, as these were people I admired and respected. I have almost ten years of online sales, and I could not ask for any better clients. These are people who really connected with my work and appreciated it. What more can I ask for?

The point that I am trying to make is that don't dismiss the oddball ventures. Be courageous. Don't follow the crowd. Gallery owners troll the internet, because artists like you and I are showing what is going on in the art studios.

As a result of my sales and exposure on eBay, I was able to move over to Ruby Lane in 2007, which is where I am now. I have sold over 1200 original works, been published a number of times and met some tremendously savvy business people - people whose business is selling online - millions of dollars a year. How better for me to learn than to be with these outstanding people? And I am proud to say that I have been able to help them too.

None of this would have happened if I listened and was intimidated by the people I respected and admired, and allowed their behaviour to modify mine.

The Key is to be Organized: Set up your computer so you can find stuff

I have my computer files organized so that I can find them easily and quickly. Here is a snapshot:

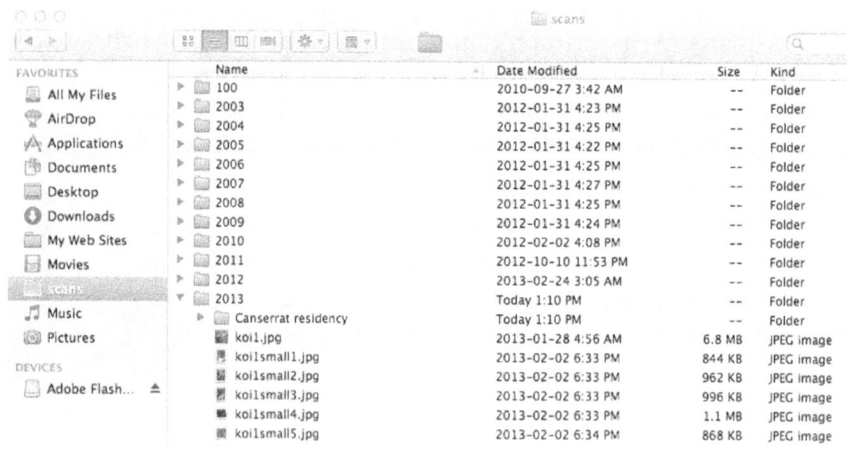

118

You can see they are listed by year, and if I have a specific project going on that year, then that project has a folder i.e. Can Serrat Residency. I have images of work done in that year in both a printable format, and a web format, with close ups for the web listings. i.e. Koi1.jpg, Koi1web.jpg etc. The best thing you can do is find a way to organize your files that makes sense to you, and stick with it.

The Internet Presence

It is the responsibility of the professional artist today to know how to use the internet. The old "I'm an artist, I don't have time to learn all that" is just plain being lazy and an excuse. In my opinion it shows an irresponsible attitude towards being able to communicate with people about your work. It is a larger world today than it was 100 years ago, and the requirements of artists have stepped up and the artists need to do the same.

These tools can include LinkedIn, Facebook, Twitter, your website, your blog, Google+, Pinterest or whatever. With today's technology, whether with a smartphone or a digital camera, there is no excuse for not being able to take pictures of your work. Much of what I do now is done with my iPhone and can be done with any phone that has a camera. There are tons of apps that allow you to crop, sharpen, brighten the images you take. It does take a small investment of your time to learn this, and anyone who says "I can't" has a defeatist and/or insecure attitude, and needs more confidence in themselves and their abilities. Find someone who can teach you. You are teachable.

If you can only do one thing, then do it well.

If you need to take a course or a workshop, do it.

Metatags

Very important to learn are metatags- aka keywords for Search Engine Optimization (SEO) - how do people on the internet find you? Through search engines, which is all keyword based.

Learn your most important keywords. Create one for yourself - of course the best built in keyword you have is your name. Run it together like I do: juliatrops. It is yours and yours alone, use it. Make it memorable. Do you have a name that other people have? Create a new one Nancy King could become nancykingart or nancykingartist or artnancyking or artistnancyking or oilsnancyking or nancykingpainting.

What would be your metatags? Brainstorm. Just write down words that have to do with your work. Things like subject, mediums, supports, where you live, your name, projects you are involved in, titles of works, all of these are great metatags.

Your List:

Big Mistake

A big mistake is to assume that once you have planted yourself in a specific internet area, that's it, your work is done. No, it is not. Places that are popular change. Remember MySpace? One thing the internet is not, is static.

Share!

Remember, the value of the internet is all in how you use it, and again, sharing is the key to the success. Keep up with your cheerleaders, join groups that have more than one or two mover and shakers. You don't have to join EVERY group. Remember that while you can't trust everyone you talk to on the internet, you can't do that in real life either. You just need to be selective and focused. Use the internet with a purpose. Set aside one hour every day just to keep up and monitor. This is hard work for some people. You have a choice - you can either roll over or you can do what you need to do.

As of 2013, the web pages you must regularly update are (not an exhaustive list) Facebook, LinkedIn, and you must have a web page or a blog. Link all these together using the social apps so you can free up time by posting one place, and it goes everywhere.

The key to the internet is sharing. Remember that the internet is a community, just as viable and important as that real life one you participate in everyday.

So share, and share freely and with an open heart. Help others, and others (ideally) will help you too.

Chapter 13 - Photographs

Photographs

Why You Need Photographs

You create the work and you need to have materials to give to people to show what you are doing. Perhaps you need to advertise for your next show, or you are sending printed images to a gallery. You will need images for the web, for your blog, for Facebook or Pinterest.

No Art is so Precious

If you are one of these artists who say that their artwork should only be experienced in person, you need to get over yourself. Everyone's art looks better in person, not just yours. The smart artists are the ones who are learning the tools to market their art effectively and with quality. If someone likes an artwork on the internet, they are likely going to love it in person. The not so smart artists are the ones who restrict the access to their work because of ego, fear and paranoia. Which artist are you?

No art is so precious that it can not go on the internet. Images are found on the internet with such great numbers that there does not seem to be any real ownership of those things visual. Media files, digital images of all sorts, from those taken directly with a camera, to those manipulated with various programs, music, video clips, all of it, the accepted standard these days is if it is on the internet, it is fair game. To protect yourself, put some sort of watermark on the image. It is not a perfect solution, but at least you have done your due diligence.

Artwork Protection and Copyright Infringements

Unless you are a visual or performing artist who has the time to chase down anyone who infringes, then if you put it up on the web, potentially you can kiss any rights goodbye. You need to understand that. If you want an image to keep its sanctity, then don't put it up. Period.

Images of the Artwork

Images are one of the most complicated things for an artist to do it seems. The problem stems from not understanding your camera. Usually, with a camera, you point it at the object, and you click the button. It is as easy as that once you get your camera set up. Learn how to do it, you won't regret the time invested.

Go to the camera shop where you bought your camera, whether London Drugs, Future Shop, Walmart etc. Tell them what you are doing - what size you need (largest or smallest), what light you are using, and ask them to set the camera up for you (ensure it is cmyk for printing, or rgb for web). Alternatively, you could read the manual, a highly recommended and effective way to spend your time. As a rule of thumb, I take the lowest resolution picture possible in rgb, because my photos are going on the web, and I don't do prints. The reason I take low resolution photos for web display is that if someone tries to take my image and print it out, it won't work so well, because pixelation occurs when the image is blown up. This is another way you can protect your work from pirates.

After the camera is set up, the most important thing is to make sure it looks good in your little window, point and shoot. Ensure your hand or the camera is supported on something solid and you won't get any fuzzies.

Two Types of Files

There are two types of files: Print and Web. The main differences between these two files are the resolution, the size and the colour panel.

1. Resolution means how many dots per square inch (confirm) are in the file.
2. Print needs more dots (pixels) and the web does not need as much. The size of the image means the actual number of pixels wide and depends on your printing requirements.
3. The colour panel has to do with the way light and colour work on the monitor and in printing. Printing requires four colours: Cyan, Magenta, Yellow and Black.

If you are interested in why this is, there are books written about the process of colour for printing and web, this is just a snapshot. For the web, there are only three colours, Red Green and Blue (think rainbows and prisms).

Taking workshops from your local photographic society would be a seriously good investment of your time and money.

For Print

Large files are required for print. By having a large file for print means that if the image is suitable for printing.

It fulfills these requirements:

a. it is 300 pixel resolution
b. it is 1500 pixels wide (dimension) minimum
c. is cmyk
d. size of actual print is dependant on needs, but aim for 5"x7"

For Web

Small files are required for the web. By having a small file for the web means that it can be viewed on the web with minimal disruption (i.e. wait time) to the web page visitor.

It fulfills these requirements:

a. it is 72 pixel resolution
b. it is 500 pixels wide (dimension)
c. is rgb.

You need images of your artwork for Calls to Artists, your blogs, your emails, your Facebook and for gallery submissions. Invest the time to learn how to take good images.

Programs I Use to Adjust Images

To create the least amount of work for yourself, take a good picture. If you take a good picture, the amount of editing you will need to do to that image is minimal, maybe even restricted to just the cropping.

The program I use if I needed to is Photoshop (PS). You don't need the latest and greatest version of Photoshop. It can be an older version such as PS 6 or 7. This will keep your cost down as well. Or you can use a free photo imaging software that comes with your computer - in a MAC it is called Preview, and in the PC is called Paint. There are other programs both free and paid available for your operating system. Do a google search on *Mac (or Windows) free image adjustment software.*

Chapter 14 - Businesses and Art

Businesses and Art

"The arts are not just a nice thing to have or to do if there is free time or if one can afford it. Rather, paintings and poetry, music and fashion, design and dialogue, they all define who we are as a people and provide an account of our history for the next generation."
Michelle Obama

Cultural Entertainment - Rant

Have you ever been contacted by an event organizer and invited to take part in their event to enrich the evening?

Usually the event organizers use words such as "exposure" or "contacts" or other hot words that indicate the artist will benefit from participation. Let me say that yes, this is all true. Events are terrific ways to get out in to the community, to help the artist decide which non profits to support and which ones have a parallel philosophy. It is important for artists to be included in cultural events, because no culture exists without art, regardless of one's own personal preferences.

However, there is a dark side to all of this. It's the "in" thing now to have artists at an event.

The common conception is that art is something you do in your "free time", and something that is not really recognized as work, so I can understand how businesses might not understand the importance of artists being paid to be present. Most of the time, we are just asked, and expected to be grateful for the "exposure". We are, but we appreciate more when you respect our skills and our time too.....

In my opinion, artists have become nothing more than free entertainment - we are asked to participate, we fill a space, we provide interaction for the attendees before, during and after, and we don't cost anything. We have become Cultural Performers. See, that is the idea with these events - they don't have to do anything for the artists because nothing has ever been done. They just ask us to be there and we jump, thinking about exposure and potential contacts and possible sales. Sometimes there is a promise of how much media will be at their event, with the promise of even more exposure. These are the carrots dangled in front of our face, and, believers in opportunity and being the eternal optimist, perhaps we take the bait, not asking any questions or making any requests.

I Think It Is Time to Make Requests

If you, as an artist, are asked to participate in an event that includes artists, or even just yourself, please ensure your name is included (at the very least!!) on the website as being at the event. They invited you specially didn't they? I know how easy it is to update a website, and adding 100 characters in the form of identities is not a hard thing to do. You are giving them your time, and if you are not being paid as the "actual" performer is, then at the very least, make sure your name is mentioned. Are you going for exposure? Then make sure the non profit fulfils their end of the bargain to ensure people know you will be there!

Even at a non-profit event you still need to be mentioned and appreciated. Are the event organizers being paid, or acknowledged as putting on the event? Are other performers being paid or acknowledged? Then why aren't you?

It can happen.

In May 2011, my fellow artist and friend Angela Bonten and I were invited to participate in Canada's Marketing Research and Intelligence Association's Annual Conference held in Kelowna. This attracted participants from all over Canada and the United States. At the conference exhibition we showcased creativity in the Okanagan, also being able to sell our work. Adding authenticity to a spectacular closing event themed French, Funky and Fruity, Angela and I were 'street artists' painting as the evening went along. It was a superbly fun evening, plus we, as artist entertainers, were paid for our time! That is business recognizing artists as business people! Finally. Thank you!

Businesses and Art

In 2010, I was on CBC Radio once again, this time talking to Daybreak South's Marion Barschel, with a fellow Kelowna resident who was involved with a highly successful music festival. I was a visual artist in the city, and at that time had been here for nine years. I was very involved in many of the cultural groups throughout those years, both visual arts and performing such as being a Board of Directors for the Kelowna Museums Society, was part of the original Life and Arts Festival Focus Group, FCA, originator of Livessence and the Okanagan Erotic Art Show, and participated with Viva Musica, the Okanagan Symphony, the Mozart Festival, Ballet Kelowna, Mission Dance Centre and Sunshine Theatre just to name a few.

The interview had to do with business and the interaction of business and culture, the premise being without business, culture will flounder, and without culture, business will stagnate. Since the CBC discussion was only about ten minutes long, and I hate to have things go to waste, here are the rest of my thoughts:

I think the biggest hurdle businesses face is recognizing that the cultural groups are as legitimate as they are. Sure, there are some artists and some groups out there that really do not put forth a "business like" attitude, but one must remember that the artists and performers are not always trained in the "Way of the Numbers". For many it is a struggle, for many they will try to overcome that struggle by learning new methods to deal with these challenges - others will just say "screw it", and hope for the best. For me, I took the initiative to learn what I could do - I know what my limitations are and what they are not. So far I haven't found too many limitations, well except for adding and subtracting. That can be a challenge sometimes. Oh, and cooking too.

The cultural health of a city could be measured, in my opinion, by the number of businesses who support the cultural groups, but more importantly, the individual artists - the larger number of businesses, the more healthy. Many businesses choose to support a cultural group via a Silent Auction, but these tend to be the same businesses over and over again - I'm sure you could name at least three here in Okanagan who do it time and again. Silent auctions, with the attendee's garage sale mentality, are an excuse to pretend to support the arts, with the minimal investment. Who really wins in this scenario? No one. The artist loses, the non profit who puts on the fund raising event loses, and the business donating a product or service is diminished publicly because their product goes for almost nothing, due to the attendee's lack of understanding of the purpose of the event with the resulting perception of the attendee being cheap.

Instead of seeing who can spend the least amount on a Silent Auction item, I'd love to see a contest on who can outdo each other, in the true nature of a fund raiser.

You know what I would like to see is a month long event, where the local businesses buy in to the concept that all art is removed from the walls. Let's just start with the art, because it's easy to administer the idea...

Remove the art from the walls for one month. Then take the temperature of the businesses and the clients/customers and the employees. Ask questions of everyone who walks in to that shop, or office, or room like how did you feel when you walked in, did it seem friendly, if it was your first time to that office could you get a sense of their philosophy (artwork displayed is a subconscious or maybe even conscious projection of that company's philosophy.) What other questions do you think you could ask? Use this opportunity to gain valuable insights from your clients/customers about your business. What a fascinating project that could be! What an opportunity to be an industry leader!

Cultural groups create from a space that is foreign from business. Artists and performers create from a space of (dare I say it) love. There is a greater good and return to money given with an open heart - something Kevin O'Leary probably wouldn't agree with.

Business and Culture, Culture is Business

Ways that traditional businesses can connect with cultural businesses:

1. Take the initiative and search out groups that you believe in from a personal and or professional point of view. Set a budget each year. Meet it. Use that interaction to show other businesses that you are taking the lead to support the culture in the city. Make it a friendly competition. By approaching cultural groups you save them incredible amounts of time, which could be translated in to presenting a much more enjoyable show, which you are supporting! Better reflection on you, right?

2. Ask the cultural groups you support to give you feedback about your donation. How much impact did it have? Ask how effective their event was. Creating accountability also creates trust – trust in you that their event will be sponsored again, and trust in them that they are being effective and efficient with the funds given and that you haven't thrown that money away.

3. Put a sign in your window or prominently on display that you support Culture! It doesn't have to be a ton of money – it could be $100, it could be $500 or it could be a stupendous amount like $10,000! (Send it my way too, please.)

Regardless of how you support the groups, just support them. We talk about tourists all the time in Okanagan because we have a tourist type town. But there are many locals who would appreciate a richer culture too. Take care of our locals, and they will tell their families, who become tourists when they visit. Then the tourists will benefit, which will mean more tourists, and a better business for you. Remember that old Brek commercial in the 70s – they'll tell two friends, and they'll tell two friends, and so on, and so on......

Chapter 15 - Spending Money

Spending Money

Spending Money

I'm an expert at spending money on art stuff. Art and art projects, whether books, shows, websites, memberships, etc are big business. We artists are multiplying like ants as everyone wakes up their creative self.

Big Business

Anything to do with art and artists is big business. Think about it. So many artists today, the market is virtually limitless. Be careful of who is trying to sell you something. Magic pills, magic galleries, magic fixes are not real. Be aware of email phishing scams to make you instantly famous, to get your artwork in front of the most influential. If it requires you to spend a lot of money i.e. more than 50$, then it is fake.

One of my favourite types of emails are those who come from website contacts, saying they saw my artwork on my site, and how wonderful it would be to include me in their "insert scheme here". When I go to the link they provide in their email, I am then requested to spend $250 or more to be included. Everything has its price, I guess.

Art Supplies: Local vs Web

It is great to support local businesses, and I try to do it myself the best way I can. I do have to take care of my own wallet however, and if I find art supplies, the same art supplies on the web for cheaper, I will order from there. The way that I see this is that it is no different from checking out sales at a local department store, or grocery store. I go where the sales are. I feel it is also the obligation of the local art stores to be competitive, to make sure they are giving the best prices possible to their local customers. Consumers are no longer restricted to the local market.On the internet, one of the best places in Canada for art supplies is Curry's in Toronto. In the States, Dick Blick is a favourite as is Jerry's Artorama.[1]

---

1   Currys.com, DickBlick.com, JerrysArtORama.com

Art Organizations

Do they really have the artists best interests at heart? This is a question only you can answer for yourself as it is a deeply personal one. I support art organizations whose goal is to support the artist, to be an advocate for the artist, and not be a political player. I deeply respect the BC Arts Council for its hard stance against the BC government when the government brought down the arts cuts. I believe that many arts organizations need to look up what it means to be an arts/artist's advocate, and determine what that definition means to them. I believe that when an arts council receives a Call to Artists asking the artists to give work away for free they should be sending it back to the originator and say no, you need to pay the artist. No more free art, we support the artist, we do not stand behind that free art philosophy.

Consider the cost to join the arts organization. Many people join just to be a member and to support the organizations overall goals. Many join to become involved in the organization. Each person decides their level of involvement. Each person decides what are the benefits the organization gives to them. Is the membership worth it?

Art Books

I love art books. I love books on other artists, especially if they have pretty pictures. I will go to them to look at, to consider, even to read. Sometimes I will take one of their artworks and do up a version of my own - this is a fairly common thing for artists to do - Picasso did it with Las Meninas, and from what I could tell, he had a lot of fun. Try it, it is liberating, and when you go back to your own work, it might even be enhanced with the subconscious assimilations from that other artist.

There will be emails you will get about art books published and you are invited to partake. Aside from the nice ego boost you get when you read their letter, consider the cost of participating. Usually there is a couple hundred dollars/pounds/euros. It is a money making venture for sure. Look up the book in the library, or look for reviews online. Are they legit? What is their purpose?

For example, I publish the catalog for the Okanagan Erotic Art Show, and do not require any further funds from the artists who were juried in the show. The reason I am doing the catalogs, which are sent to the National Library in Canada, is to make a permanent record of the show, so that in ten years, when an art historian goes looking for the status of erotic art, or even art in the Okanagan, the catalogs will come up. These are records, accurate records of what was displayed (not necessarily accepted) in our area.

Art Shows

So many art shows, so little time! A good source for art shows is CaFE and Zapplication.[2] Another good sources is Professional Artist magazine, which also lists free Call to Artists. Consider the cost of the artwork submission, and also the shipping to and from the place if the show is not local. Consider customs and other border fees.

Beware of the Art Shows that take advantage of the name recognition of other established art shows. I am referring to the Biennales that have popped up in various countries. There is only one recognized Art Biennale and that is in Venice. Look at the costs that are involved. Look at the returns you will get. Let common sense be your guide.

Art Websites

So many artist websites to show and sell work, it is impossible to list them all. The more popular ones are Etsy, DeviantArt, RubyLane (where I am), FineArtAmerica, are the ones that come top of mind. Many of the google groups are a great place to show work, just look for one that fits your subject matter. Some you will need to request approval to join, don't let that put you off. Many people just use Facebook, or Instagram, or Pinterest, or Flickr. All are good. Go where you are comfortable.

With a little bit of work, you can sell your work from your own website, by adding a paypal button, or sell from your Facebook fan page.

---

2   http://www.CallforEntries.org and http://www.zapplication.org

Art Residencies

There are two art residency websites that I monitor. One is ResArtis. org and the other is ArtistCommunities.org. Why am I an advocate for residencies? Because you get out of your comfort zone, you get out in the world, you meet new people, you get recharged. You learn something from where you are and you learn something about yourself. Costs vary from free to a paid stipend, to 1000$ a month to $5000 a month. Consider the pros and cons. Is there a place on your bucket list that you would like to go? Try to do it through an artist residency. You get to work, and play and you meet people from around the world who have the same love as you, art.

If you are returning overseas or on a flight, artwork can be couriered through by you, as carry on luggage. I recently returned with some huge canvases from Spain, and used the large tubes to carry them unstretched. Check your airline's requirements. Always declare what you have. Don't try to fool around with the Border Security.

Shipping of Artwork

There's lots of things to think about when you are shipping artwork. My preference for shipper currently is Canada Post or USPS. If brokerage is not done correctly between Canada and the US, the artist can expect to pay through the nose. Depending on value of work, and location of purchaser, my first choices for shipping would be Post, then Fedex.

I pack my own work. I try not to ship glass if at all possible. Drawings are shipped unframed, unmatted (usually), secured between two sheets of coroplast. Canvases up to 30"x40" are shipped stretched in a hand made box. Anything over that is shipped unstretched in a tube. Having said that, however, there is a new manufacturer of stretched canvas called Genie Canvas. The inventor, Mike Schwed from New York State, has created a system where up to 4 feet by 6 feet can be reduced down to a shippable size. Check him out at http://www.geniecanvas. com. I've tried them, and they are brilliant. Easy to take plein-air! If you do end up ordering, please tell him of this referral, I would receive a 5% commission.

144

Case Study

In June, for the 2013 Okanagan Erotic Art Show, one of the accepted artists was Victoria Pendragon from West Virginia. Victoria used her local UPS store to have the work shipped to me in Canada. In order for me to take possession of this unsold artwork, Victoria was required to pay an additional $111.90 in Canadian taxes. She would not have been charged if the paperwork was processed correctly by the shipper.

When I went to the border later on, I asked why these charges were levied. The Border Patrol Officer said that based on her paperwork in her package, she did everything correctly, but the brokerage was not done as her forms were not signed. I spoke to the Border Control personally and we reviewed all the information presented from UPS and from Victoria. As well, he said because the artwork was not processed properly to leave the States, potentially she could have been charged to have the artwork returned to her in the States. Note that this is in addition to the $40.61 that she paid just to have the work shipped to me.

CanadaPost rates are more expensive than USPS, and to return the work to her, it would have cost about $50 through CanadaPost, including tracking for 5-7 day service. I had seven other US artists who needed work returned (all had used USPS and had no problems) so I made the trip to the border which was about two hours away. Her return shipping was just under $20 for the two day service. I had her forms stamped to show that the work returned to the States through the border, and also included the forms that she needs to reclaim those Canadian taxes. I am not sure she will get them back through, because that crucial original paperwork was not done. That's quite a difference in costs, right? All the costs are online, so go to the shipper's website, and enter the dimensions of the package, and do your comparison.

Check the regulations of the country you need to ship to and consider what it would cost for the works to come back. Look to see what paperwork you need. Factor those prices in to your budget to see if it is worth participating in the show. Maybe the show will be a good CV entry, and so can be justified. Sending work across the border can be easy, you just need to follow the protocol.

Chapter 16 - The Artist and the City

The Artist and the City

As a visual artist, or a performer, a writer, a musician, you live within a community. It is not enough anymore to say I'm an artist, here is my art. If you are interested in making a successful art career, you need to interact with the local community too. Sure, there are going to be the few people who say that they don't, that they prefer to be by themselves, they're hermits, they are anti-social, or other such reasons why they do not want to be involved in their community, and that's fine, and I respect that.

The other people who say that they live within a community and they want to contribute to their community, regardless of how small a way, I respect that too. I respect that more however, because this kind of interaction is one that encourages us all to grow, and grow together. The world is a big place, and regardless of how small we wish it were, it is no longer. We need each other to live, to survive, and that contrast of human interaction is what softens our edges or creates new ones. Safety and seclusion does have its time and space, but in my opinion, for the socially conscious artist, there should be some sort of balance of activity.

When I arrived in Kelowna in 2001, I won a spot at the newly built Rotary Centre for the Arts (RCA), the public space funded by the artists and performers in the city, and also by grants from the City. Because there was so much of the local populace invested in the building and the concept of the building, and I was going to be having a studio in this wonderful building, I felt that it was necessary for me to give back too. There is a saying that the world doesn't owe you, you owe the world. This is how I have lived my life.

Having been involved in the City of Kelowna and the Okanagan for over ten years, I have learned that art is for those who are interested and art is for those who are not sure if they are interested. It seems to be a simplistic sentence, but let me assure you that while many people are interested, there are many more who are intimidated and if it were not for the intimidation, or the feeling of not being welcome, or being "smart enough" for art, they would be in there like dirty shirts.

What Kinds of Things?

The City of Kelowna, in my opinion, has done much to try to bridge the gap for the public and the artist, with the RCA being an instrumental part of that district. The Cultural District was one initiative where the City had created a place for the artists and performers to create art and perform. This is located downtown just north of the core. This location has been criticized by many as not the most ideal, and there are many critics who say that the art and performances do not only happen downtown. They are correct. Creativity is something that happens even in your own backyard, with landscaping and with the choosing and placement of garden sculptures.

Things you can do to get involved is apply to sit on the boards for a non profit association like the art gallery, the museum, a health charity you believe in, a children's charity you believe in, the list goes on. Put on workshops for them. Partner with other groups, other artists.

So many people I have met while in the studio at the RCA or on the boards I've served on, said they wished they could draw or paint or sing or perform. Well, they can. It is just them that holds them back, just as it is our own selves that hold us back from our own aspirations.

All is Art, All is Creative

Encourage your friends to think outside the box of what art is, and you will find that interaction will increase within the general population of the city. Point out whenever they do something creative, or surpass a limitation or boundary. More people will find themselves able and willing and have the courage to participate in activities and events, and even feel comfortable enough to purchase a work. There are no losers in this education process!

Here is an example of the education process in action, on more of a strategic level, but the filtering down will have some fabulous results, I am sure.

Find Out About the City's Initiatives

Kelowna puts on Summits: get togethers that include all sorts of creative types from the Okanagan. Usually they include board members from the cultural entities like the art gallery, museum, theatre groups, musical groups and such, and sometimes, artists individually will be invited.

June 2013, I participated in the latest City of Kelowna Cultural Summit, called From Volume to Value: Building Engagement, Capacity and Resilience. The first day topic was Public Engagement: Building and Measuring Impact. While the Summit itself was centered around the non profit sector, and I attended as part of my position on the Kelowna Museums Society board, I could definitely see the application of these principles to the artist as a sole entrepreneur. As you read through these, consider that this is more of the community as a whole focus, but see how you can apply these comments and thoughts to your own practice.

The first speaker was Howard Jang, from the Canada Council for the Arts, and he spoke about access to the arts being vital to cultural citizenship and building vital communities. His comments are definitely applicable to the non profit sector, but also to the artist.

The Dialog

Anytime you interact with someone, including yourself critically, there is a dialog. We are mission driven. Whether we create for ourselves, or for another, we have a goal, and that is to express. The motives behind that goal can be altruistic, or they can be entrepreneurial. It doesn't matter. It is enough for some to have these creations for themselves, this might be their secret life, but for most of us, we want to share our expressions with our friends and our family, depending on how supportive they are, perhaps we share them with our favourite charity. Perhaps we just share them with the public under an assumed name for fear of criticism, but unless these creations are part of our secret life, we share them... somehow.

We are expressing something, so what is the message that we want to give or present? Can we get this message across to someone we've never met? Whatever we are doing is important to us, and we want to share - for some of us, we need to share, it is just part of our personality. Sharing allows us to get feedback on the success of our message - whatever that message is, and also creates a platform for a dialog to happen between you the creator, and them, the audience.

The dialog is what encourages us to grow. Growth is not always comfortable though, in fact it seldom is, but it is necessary. Questions that can be partially answered through this dialog include what is the real meaning and value of what we do?

How To Have That Conversation

Create an environment for discussion, and decide what language to use. If you use language that only a select number of people can understand then expect that level of involvement. Language can be the number one facilitator or the number one barrier. Use language that is friendly, and welcoming.

152

Participate in Cultural Events Put on by the City

Technology > Isolation > Return to Centre > Community

Engagement is a multi level platform. One thing I thought about when I heard him say this is that there are more ways to communicate to a person than just the visual or the verbal. With so much focus on technology, there is a lack of understanding or appreciation for the in person, one on one contact.

We artists generally live and work in isolation, we need to get back to our centre, the heart of ourselves, and the heart of our community. One way we do that is by art shows. Art shows are not just to be held for a special few, usually the same few from show to show or venue to venue, but to be open to all. There should be no intimidation or limitation for those artists who are interested. This is one lesson learned from the institution called the church, and regardless of your religious beliefs, visual art was the primary method of delivery of communication, and instruction, and that accessibility to these visual icons were re-presented constantly. Participate in the city's cultural events, and get your work out in to the community, your community.

Come to the Experience Prepared

Whether for an art show, an open studio or whatever you participate in, have your documents completed. For the artist, that means the CV, the Biography and the Artist Statement. Don't be afraid to talk about yourself, what your interests are. You are your brand. You are a verb. The client will be captured as much by the story of you as by the image of your artworks.

Discuss your works in the show. Does your work captivate? What attracted them to it? Tell them, and then tell them again, and then let them experience what you told them about. Point out specifics, if you have them. Relay experiences from when you were creating the work. Explain your vision even though it can be unexplainable.. Find the language that will encourage community participation. It is your responsibility to encourage and provide ways to engage your community.   153

What you are doing when you create an environment for discussion is that you are creating your own arts eco-system, one that is based on you and your role as an artist, and your work as the life within.

There are many ways to engage the community. Inviting community to your place starts the conversation. The attendee might have just happened upon your studio or your show, or the attendee planned on coming to your studio or show. Either way, you have an attendee at your studio or your show. Engage them. Welcome them in to your arts eco-system. Be inclusive.

"To foster and promote the study and enjoyment of and the production of works in the arts."
Canada Council for the Arts

Any time you participate in a community event as an artist, consider having this as your mandate, your mission. Sure your ultimate goal might be to sell your artworks, but until that happens, encourage people to enjoy what is on display. Don't underestimate the influence of even two or three people. You never know what will come out.

Summary

If your city has a cultural department, look them up and see what they are doing. Contact them to find out how you can get involved and further their mandate, which ultimately is yours. If your city does not have a cultural department, perhaps it is the arts council that leads the way in the creative sector. Get involved with them. Be inclusive for all artists. Leave no one behind.

It is the artist who, according to Joseph Campbell, is the Shaman of our society and the one who will pull our society back together.

Chapter 17 - Creating Your Event

Creating your event

The last chapter of this book will outline how to put on an event, which can be anything - an art show, a costume party, whatever you wish. This is the template that I created out of necessity and follow when putting together the Okanagan Erotic Art Show.

Focus

The first question you want to ask yourself is what is your motivation for putting on this event. Are you reacting against something, want to bring something to light, want to showcase a specific subject? It can be anything. Want to just have a party and get people together to look at art? Sure. Anything goes. So decide what your focus is, and start to build around it.

Case Study

I'm going to give you the background of the Okanagan Erotic Art Show, because that is what I am involved with presently, and I think it's pretty successful. Any dates that you see in the notes on the following pages have to do with the 2013 show, and things that I noted to be in order for 2014. Each year I try to put out a better show. You could take your focus, and then adapt all the headings that follow to make it relevant to your show or event.

Here is the preface of the Okanagan Erotic Art Show Catalog, a publication I put out every year for the show:

"The Okanagan Erotic Show emerged in 2007, fellow artists Lauren Wilson, Angela Hansen and myself were talking about having an art show that was a bit more exciting than the usual run of the mill life drawing exhibitions. We were having a sip (or two, maybe more, I can't remember) of wine while manning the Livessence booth at one of the local art shows, and noticed there were many people who would barely glance at the nudes on display. Censorship about what was "proper" had reared its ugly head. Knowing full well that erotic is perceived individually, we wanted to shake things up. We wanted to have some FUN!

The first show, "Blush, what makes you?" at the Rotary Centre for the Arts (RCA) in 2008 was a huge success, but as you can imagine, as the RCA is a public building, there were a few complaints. In 2009, Angela went on to have her first child, and Lauren went traveling in Asia, so that year, I carried on my own, and have since.

"Raw......Whispers" was at A. Woodside Design Gallery, and that year I created the first catalog. I realized how important that record seemed to be to each artist and I had fun doing it.

2010 saw a bit of rough bumps and grinds, but that experience showed me where we, the Okanagan artists, were in terms of comfort level and where we, the local public, were in terms of artistic support and adventure. "Seduce Me" (2010), "The Edge of Night" (2011) and "Rumour has it..." (2012) were held at a new winery, Ex Nihilo Vineyards in Lake Country. I was overwhelmed by the attendance at the opening nights, and the tremendously positive comments on the show throughout its run. Each year it increased in popularity and attendance with almost 300 attendees in 2012 at opening night, and many of the artists, and patrons, dressed up!

Every year I chose a charity to support from the show. The first three years I did this was the Canadian Breast Cancer Society, with amost $3000 donated. The charity chosen for 2012 and 2013 is the Central Okanagan Hospice Association, in memory of Tracie Ward, the Executive Director of the Rotary Centre for the Arts from 2005 - 2012. Over these two years, almost $4500 was donated to the Hospice Association. Tracie was the first champion of the first Erotic Show and in spite of the negative comments received, her view was that the RCA is an Arts Centre first and foremost. Thank you Tracie!

At the 2012 Opening Night, I was approached by Hans-Peter Mayr, General Manager and CEO of Sparkling Hills Resort, who indicated he would be interested in presenting the show. 2013 saw a new and exciting venue, the artworks were placed in the Ballroom and the Fireside Lounge, scrumptious appetizers and wine was provided by Sparkling Hill. I arranged entertainment representing a few of the creative disciplines which included theatre, music and dance.

In 2013, I also ensured that the public knew that the Opening Night was costume encouraged but not mandatory. So many of them came in costume and masks, so many smiling faces. It was a party, an art opening where the idea of not knowing the next person but still being able to talk to them was important, so different than the stiff, staid openings that I had been to in the past. This is what it should be about, having fun, looking at art. Over 330 people attended the ticketed Opening Night. It is an event where the people who attended became part of the show.

Over the past six years, I've fine tuned the procedures, categories of action, and steps to make the show organized and a success. Here are my notes as to how things needed to be decided. This is for an art show event, but you could probably use this template to put on any event. Again, the dates as shown here are for the 2013 UnSpoken Secrets held at Sparkling Hill Resort July 4 to Aug 2.

Date of Event
July 2013
Potential show run - July 5 to August 2

Theme
UnSpoken Secrets - based on Phantom of the Opera's song, Past the Point of No Return

Public Relations
PR to do with the host, will be through the host
PR to do with the art show, will be through me
The host will place the Call and the show event on their website
I will take care of the Art Show website
Each artist to do blog article for their piece

Juried Show
Theme to be determined
Jury = myself and potentially two other artists/art related/business people

Submissions Assistant
Submissions Assistant worked well

Call to Artists

Dec 1 to March 15

Jurying complete March 20

Notifications to artists by March 22

Artists will be required to provide easels if oversize, and insurance on the works.

Artists will take care of transportation to and from the host

Artwork will be delivered to the Resort between June 24 and July 4

Maximum 75 artworks

Size limitation, no larger than 36" longest side

Instructions for Jury

Each juror gets one vote per artwork

Jurying is done blind ie no names

Each "yes"=1, "maybe" =.5 and "no"=0

Artworks with 2 points are juried in up to max of 75

Discretion ie those with 1.5 remains with organizer to fill 75

Setup

Thursday July 4 10 am-3 pm

Artwork labels need to be on glossy index card stock

Grid cubes worked well

One artwork per grid

Zap straps for security worked well

Display

On easels and grids

Location to be determined at host facility

When there are weddings booked on Saturday, artworks will be moved out of the ballroom by host staff Friday evening, and replaced Sunday morning

I will provide labels, signage

I can create a small map specific to the show

I may need lights, which I will supply

Vernissage
Friday evening, July 5, ticketed, $30, at door $40, masquerade type
350 max tickets including 50 comps
Comps: 10 to host, remainder for Gallery Hosts, Press & Performers
1/3 ticket price to host
1/3 ticket price to me
1/3 ticket price to charity
Catering and Wine provided by host
M/C - personality dependant on theme
Bar - cash bar only

Tickets
Tickets will include one glass of wine, and a people's choice ballot
Have tickets available for purchase online immediately
Include the paypal fees for tickets on the online purchase button
No credit card ticket purchases at the door, cash only
Two sets of people (4) handling people coming in

Performers
Vignettes throughout the evening, music, dance, theatre
Outline of the evening to be determined March 2013
No vulgarity

Photographer
Hire a photographer (paid) to take pics throughout the evening, give him/her a comp ticket
Photographer to take pics of guests as they come through the door
Photographer provides web photos, printed photos guests to contact him directly

Press Passes
Have press passes available, max 10
Photographers need to provide me with minimum of ten photos
Writers need to send back article

People's Choice
Have ballot box on ticket table
Count ballots every 15 minutes
Have deadline time 15 minutes prior to announcement time

Prizes
I will pay the cash prize of $250 for People's Choice and the Resort Choice out of Call to Artist Submissions

The host will need to pick their favourite artwork from the successful pieces once the show is set up

Receipt for cash prizes

Signage
Important: make maps and signs for each floor/ elevator

Catalog
I will create the catalog for the art show

It does not cost the juried artist or the host to be in the catalog

The catalog goes to the National Library and Archives in Canada

The host will receive a complementary copy of the catalog

The host can be featured in the catalog, this article is written by the host and sent to me by the deadline. Topics can be why you were interested in having the art show at the Resort, what your thoughts are on the artworks that will be presented ... any and or all the above

Host to provide a printable logo for posters and the catalog

Catalogs can be sold at the Resort and price will be worked out after the Catalog is complete

If the host sells the catalog, they made the $5 per book

If I sold the catalog, I made the $5 per book

Gallery Hours
Hours open to the public 10-6 daily

Needs a gallery host for the day

Gallery Hosts
Artists are welcome to be Gallery Hosts for the show run

Make up list for gallery host to introduce show, theme, artist statements, locations, how many artists, pieces, where from

They will pay for their Opening Night ticket, and be reimbursed when they do their shift

Artist to get their own nametags: Exhibiting Artist or name

Shift is 10-6 pm

Sales of Artwork
The Resort will take sales of artwork with 30% commission
Sales will be paid to the artist by the end of the show.

Blog
Blog about where the show is and why
Remind artists this is THEIR show, and they need to do work too

Take Down
Monday August 5 10 am - 3 pm
Artists to tell me when they are coming to pick up their work, time/ date

Items to Bring for Setup
Set up took from 9 am to about 3 pm.
signs
grids,
easels
easels for signs
printing
labels
lights
catalogs
zap straps
cutters
tape - green, black, clear
wrap for sold artwork
stamp for hands
stamp pad
extension cords
plastic stands
posters mounted on coroplast
tools: screwdriver, cutter, wire, allen keys
electrical tape in four colours to colour code areas
donation box
pens
highlighters
bulldog clips (small)
envelopes

Printing

tickets 350 (50 volunteer), same design as 2013
add no refunds on front
ticket list (two for table, one for photographer)
people's choice & inventory list (300 for month)
maps for artwork for resort
maps for artwork for volunteers
posters
catalog poster
donation box poster
list of people who ordered catalogs (paid and not paid)
Opening night table instructions

Summary

This is pretty much what I go through each year, coordinating the event so that while Murphy is invited, he doesn't show up. I start this planning process about a month prior to the Call to Artists going out. For the 2013 show, I started it in November in order to launch the Call to Artists December 1, with the actual show in July. It is a lot of work so be prepared for that. While my list is comprehensive, and I made an effort not to leave anything out, things that have become automatic might not be included.

During the time for the Call, I usually get a lot of questions on the show, what the theme is, when it is, what type of work is accepted etc, which are all answered on the website http://www.OkanaganEroticArtShow. com, either in the main post on the page, the graphic at the top, or the FAQ page. Yet still I get questions. I am making it a habit not to waste time anymore on the questions already answered on the website.

You can now see where I get some of my experience in dealing with shows, and artists and what really works. As I stated in the beginning of the book, read this information, and choose what works for you.

Chapter 18 - Summary

Summary

As a professional artist, art is a business. Structure and planning is important. Pathways for the future also known as a business plan or direction is important. Where do you want to be in ten years? Do you need to be paid? You have to ask yourself are you worth it. You have to decide if you are worth it.

There's a fine line for artwork sales and integrity and it goes all away from getting up in the morning to going to bed. You need to feel good about what, why and how you are living your life.

One Final Piece of Wisdom?

If I had one piece of wisdom to pass on to people struggling with art and the "real world", what would I tell them?

Learn self-discipline, time management, and tell anyone who says you can't do "something" to screw off. Don't take no for an answer. If you can think it, you can do it. Be adaptable. Find your own solutions to problems. Make your own rules. Take responsibility for your life, your work and your thoughts. Be adaptable. Do not avoid struggling as there is nothing wrong with it, it is the heart of creative thinking. Fail. Get back up. Be adaptable. Face your shadow and your demons, they are a rich treasure of understanding and inspiration.

Okay, guess that's more than one.

And Lastly

This book could not be written without the love and support of many people. From the bottom of my heart, I thank my family, my friends including those who are not local, and my clients. You are the best cheerleaders ever.

Appendix 1 - Recommended Reading

(not an exhaustive list)

Self-Reliance, Sir Ralph Waldo Emerson

The Business Side of Creativity, Cameron S Foote

Making a Living as an Artist, The Editors of Art Calendar

Art Marketing 101, Constance Smith

Messages from the Real World, Ted Godwin

Julia Cameron, The Artist's Way

But is it Art, Cynthia Freeland

Steal like an Artist, Austin Kleon

Manage Your Day-to-Day: Build Your Routine, Find Your Focus, and Sharpen Your Creative Mind (The 99U Book Series)

Appendix 2 - Arts Funders in Canada (2013)[1]

2010 Legacies Now, Arts Now
Alberta Foundation for the Arts
Atlantic Canada Opportunities Agency
B.C. Arts Council
B.C. Capital Regional District
Calgary Arts Development Authority
Canadian Heritage – Atlantic Region
Canadian Heritage – Prairies and Northern Region
Canadian Heritage – Strategic Policy and Research Branch
Canadian Heritage – Western Region
City of Charlottetown
City of Kelowna
City of St. John's
City of Vancouver, Cultural Services
City of Yellowknife
Conseil des Arts et des Lettres du Québec
Edmonton Arts Council
Government of Alberta – Tourism, Parks, Recreation and Culture
Government of British Columbia – B.C. Cultural Services Branch
Government of Manitoba – Culture, Heritage and Tourism
Government of Newfoundland and Labrador – Tourism, Culture and Recreation
Government of Nova Scotia – Tourism, Culture and Heritage
Government of Prince Edward Island – Community and Cultural Affairs
Government of the Northwest Territories – Education, Culture and Employment
Government of the Northwest Territories Industry, Tourism and Investment
Government of Yukon Tourism and Culture and Yukon Arts Advisory Council
Greater Vancouver Regional District
Halifax Regional Council
Halifax Regional Municipality
Manitoba Arts Council
New Brunswick Arts Board
Newfoundland and Labrador Arts Council
Newfoundland and Labrador Film Development Corporation
Newfoundland and Labrador Music Industry Association
Northwest Territories Arts Council
Nova Scotia Arts and Culture Partnership Council
Ontario Arts Council
Prince Edward Island Council of the Arts
Saskatchewan Arts Board
Service Canada, Newfoundland and Labrador
Vancouver Foundation
Vancouver Organizing Committee for the 2010 Olympic and Paralympic Games
Winnipeg Arts Council
Winnipeg Foundation

www.ingramcontent.com/pod-product-compliance
Lightning Source LLC
Chambersburg PA
CBHW060848170526
45158CB00001B/272